Dear O.B.D,
This is a gratitude to life, a tribute to the divine that guides our steps. I thank God
for all the blessings and, above all, for placing you in my path. I believe that the
true purpose of existence is to give meaning to the lives around us, and you, dear
O.B.D, are the deepest meaning of my journey.
Your love fills every empty space, brightens every shadow, and adds color to
every moment. You are the reason why my life has such a special purpose.
Loving you is a divine gift, and for that, I express my gratitude to God for placing
you at the center of my heart.
With all my love,

David Lucas
2024

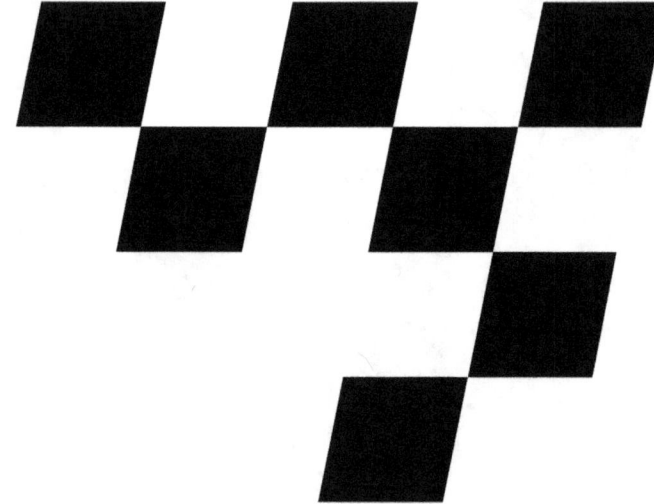

This Book Belongs to:

○────────────────────────────────────○

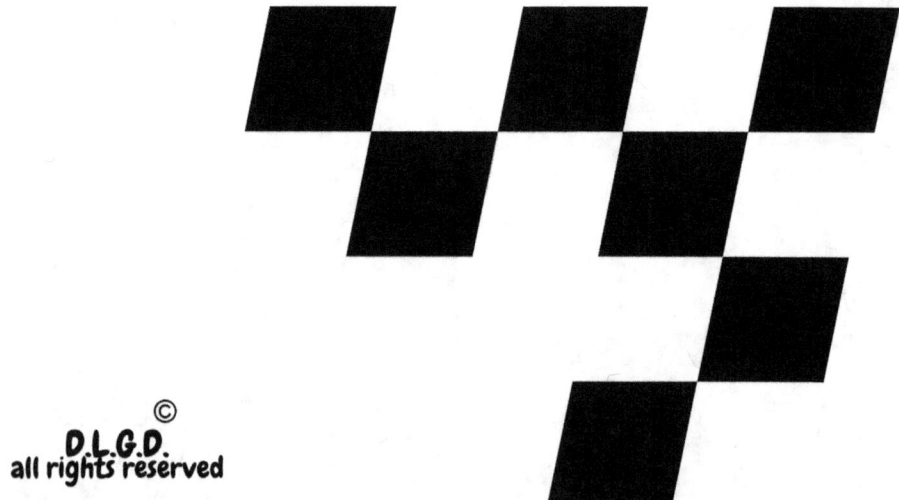

Test Color Page

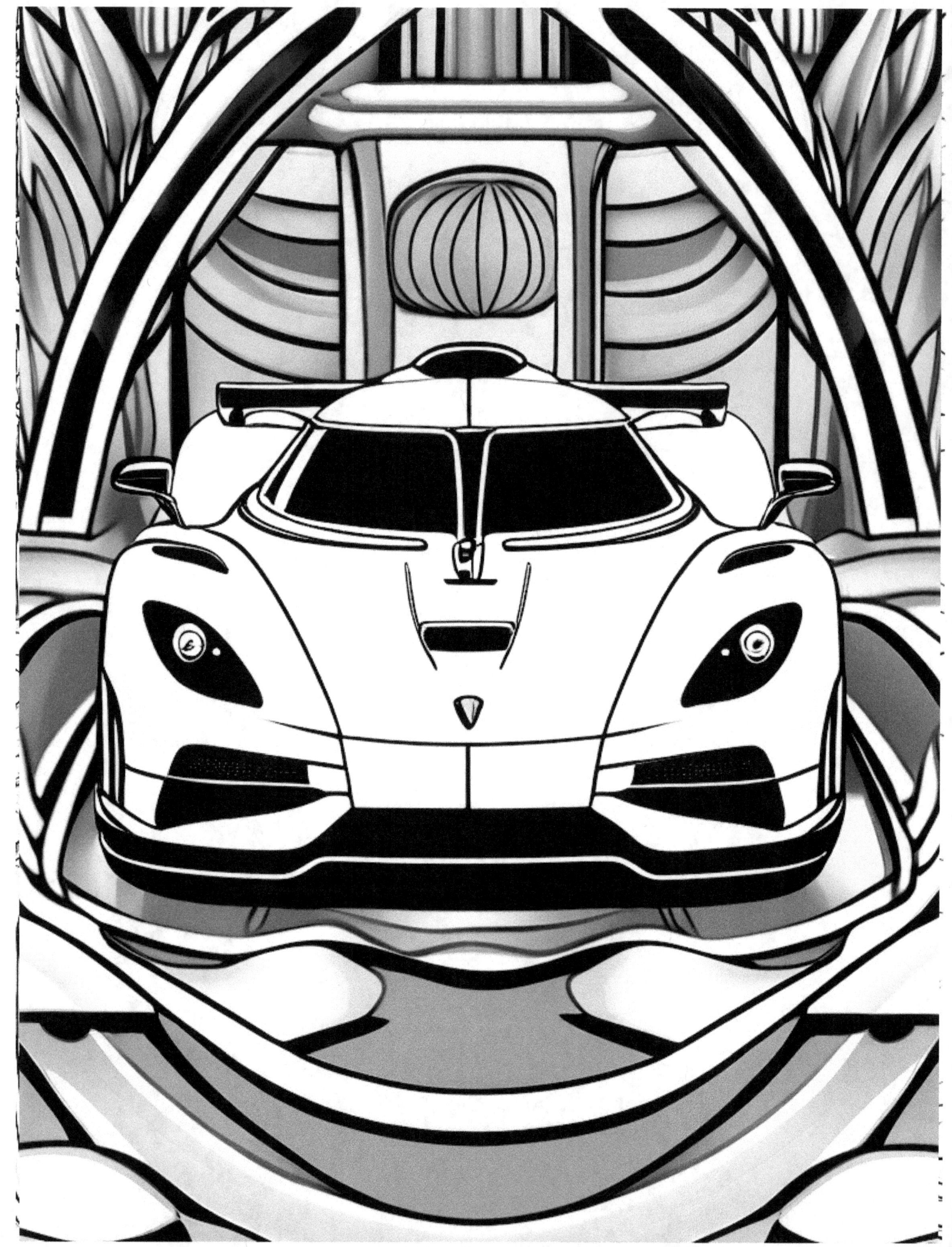

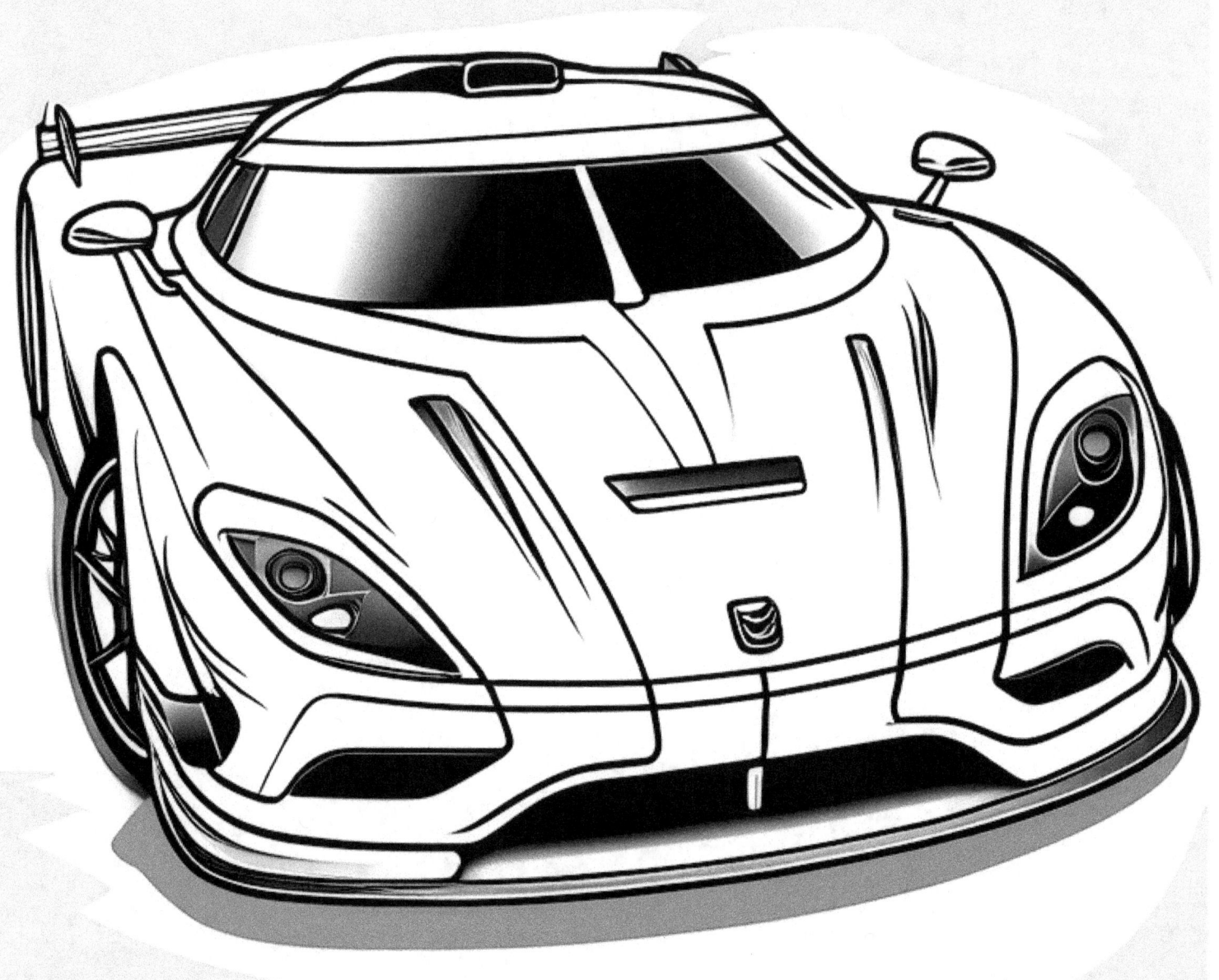

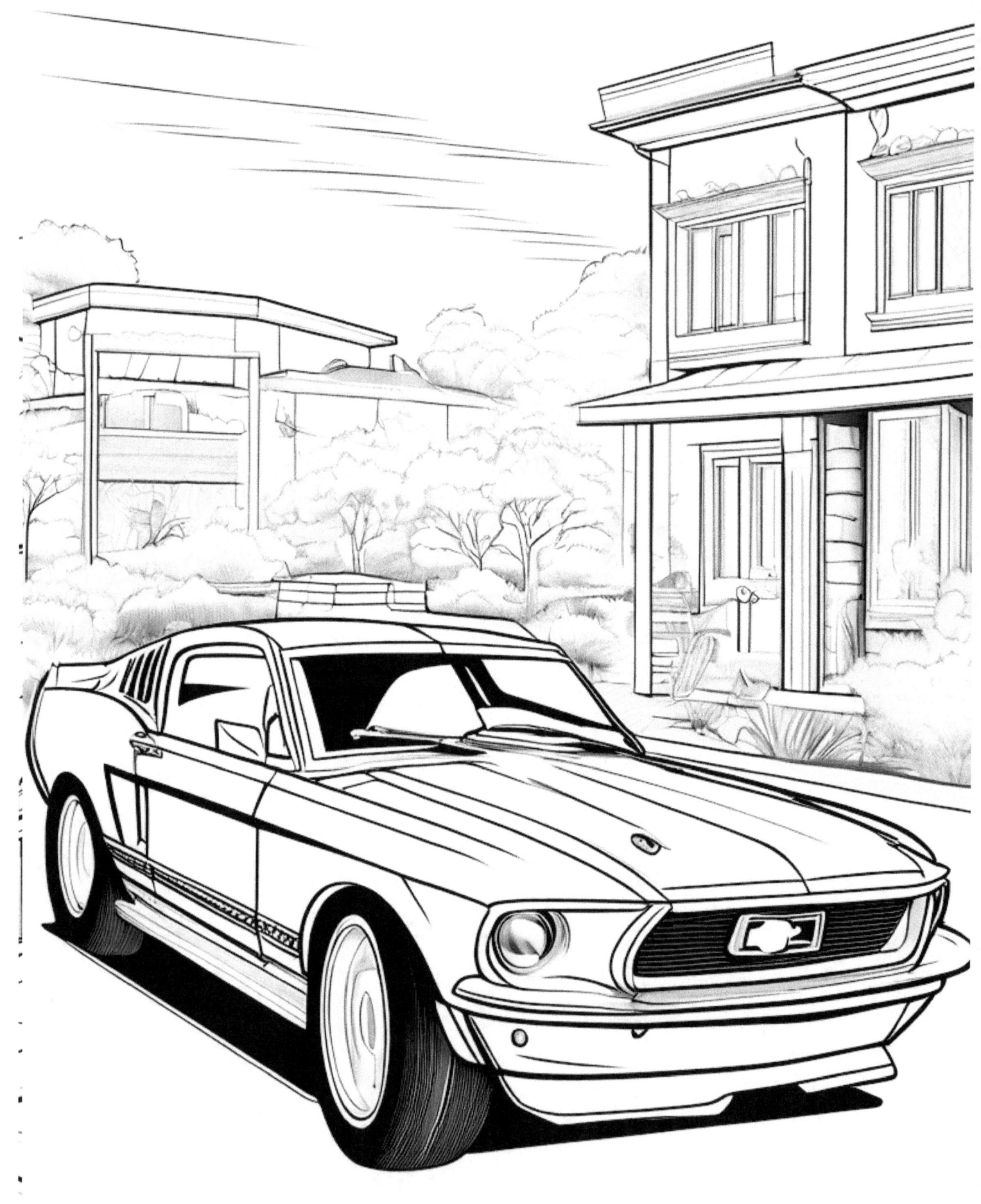

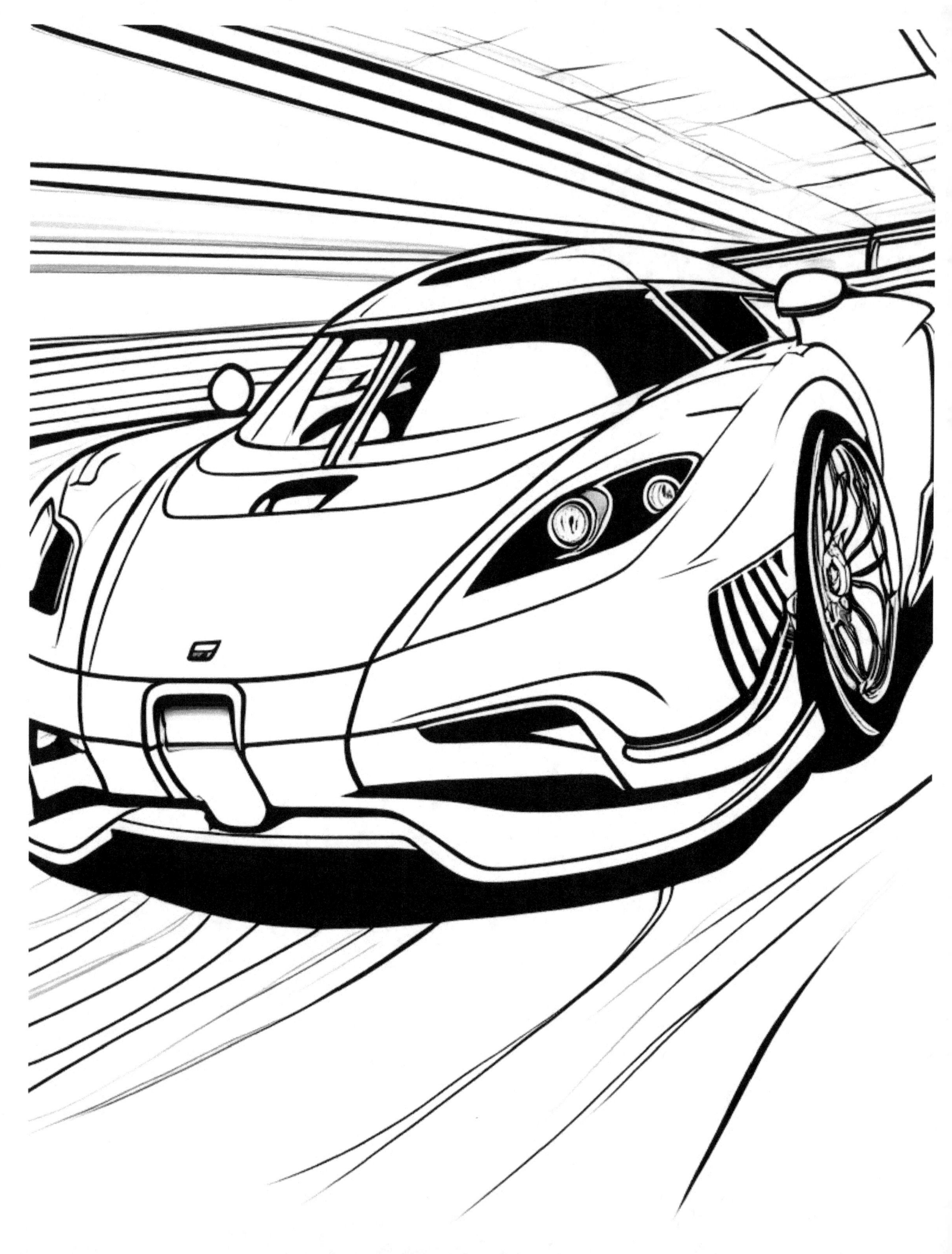

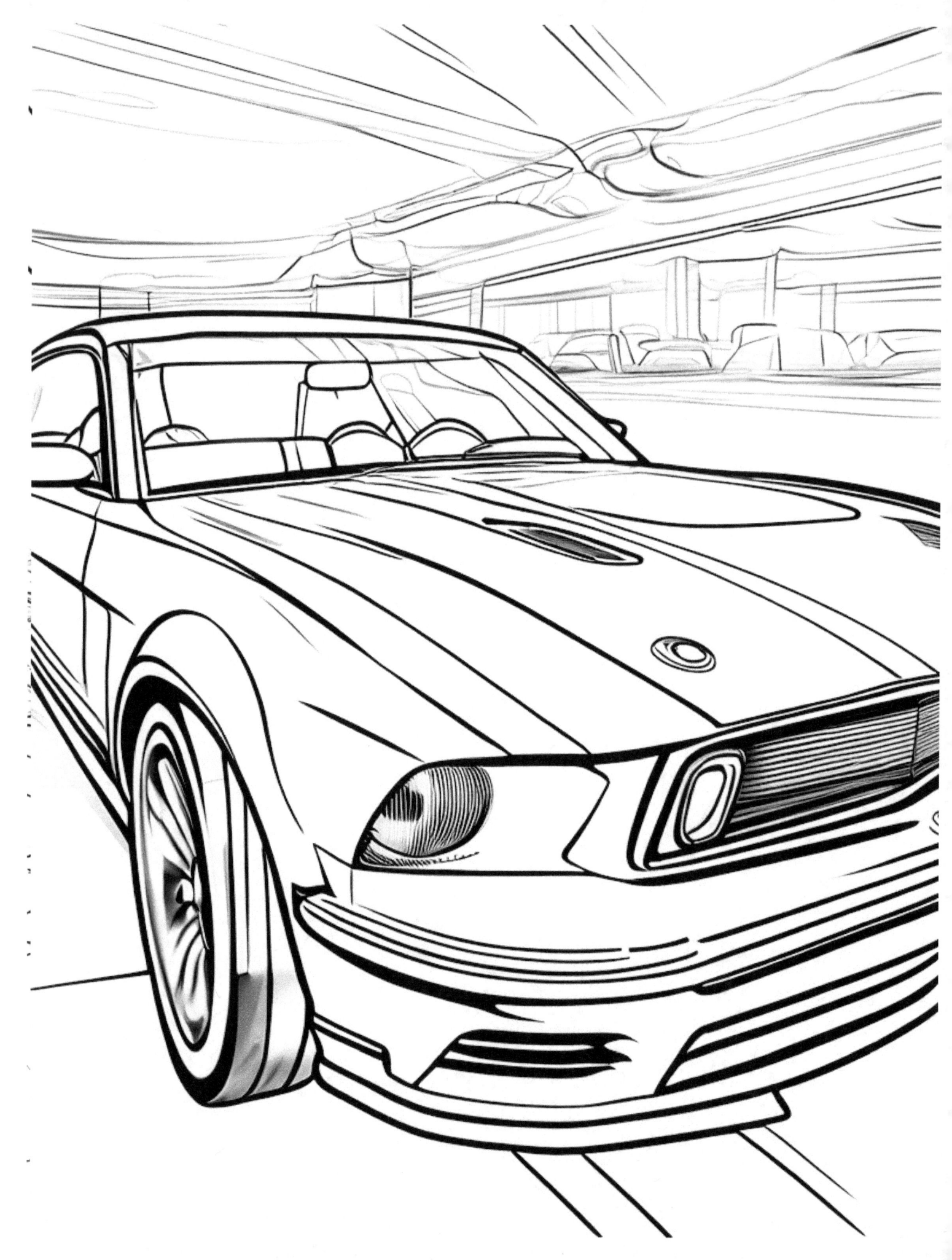

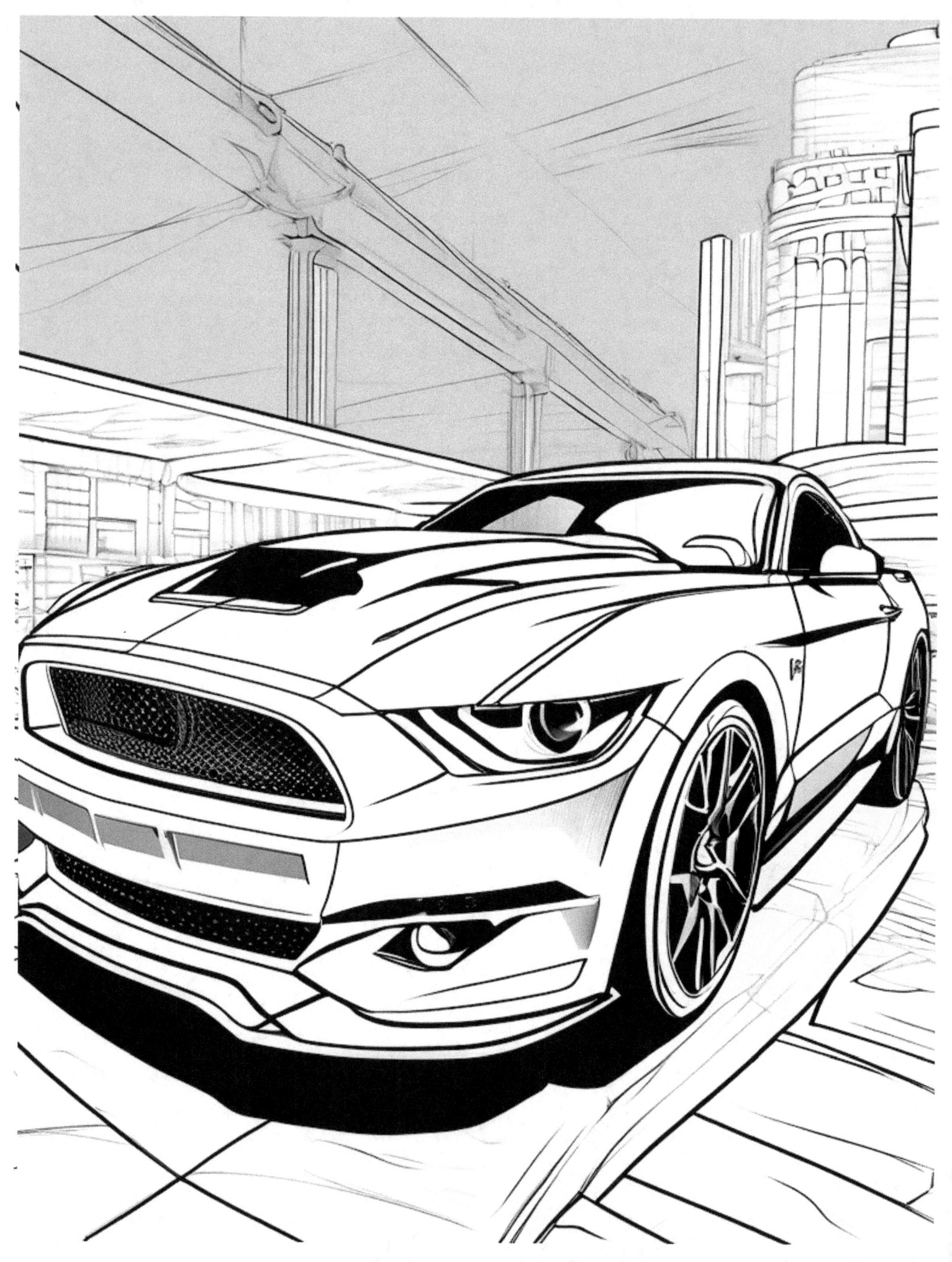

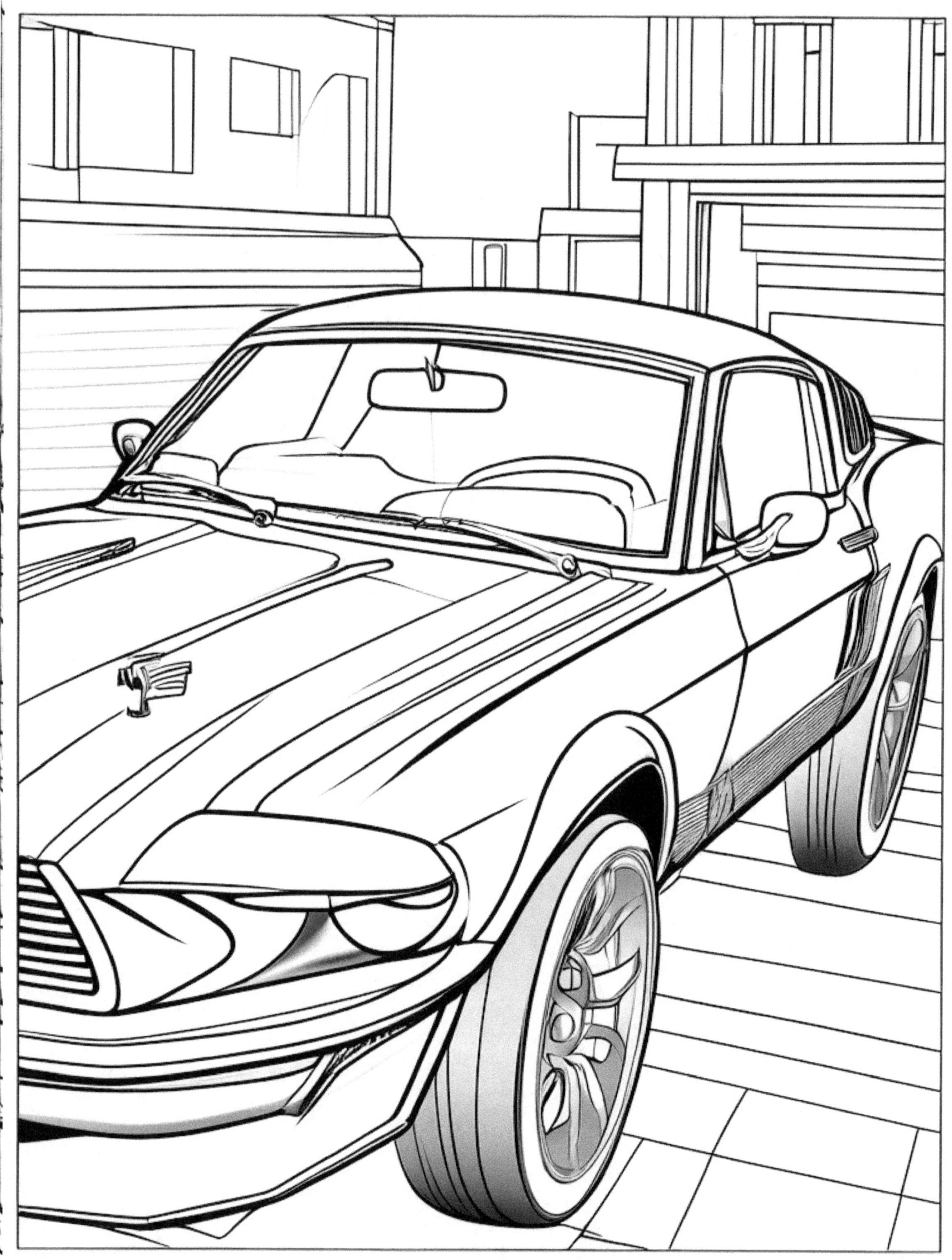

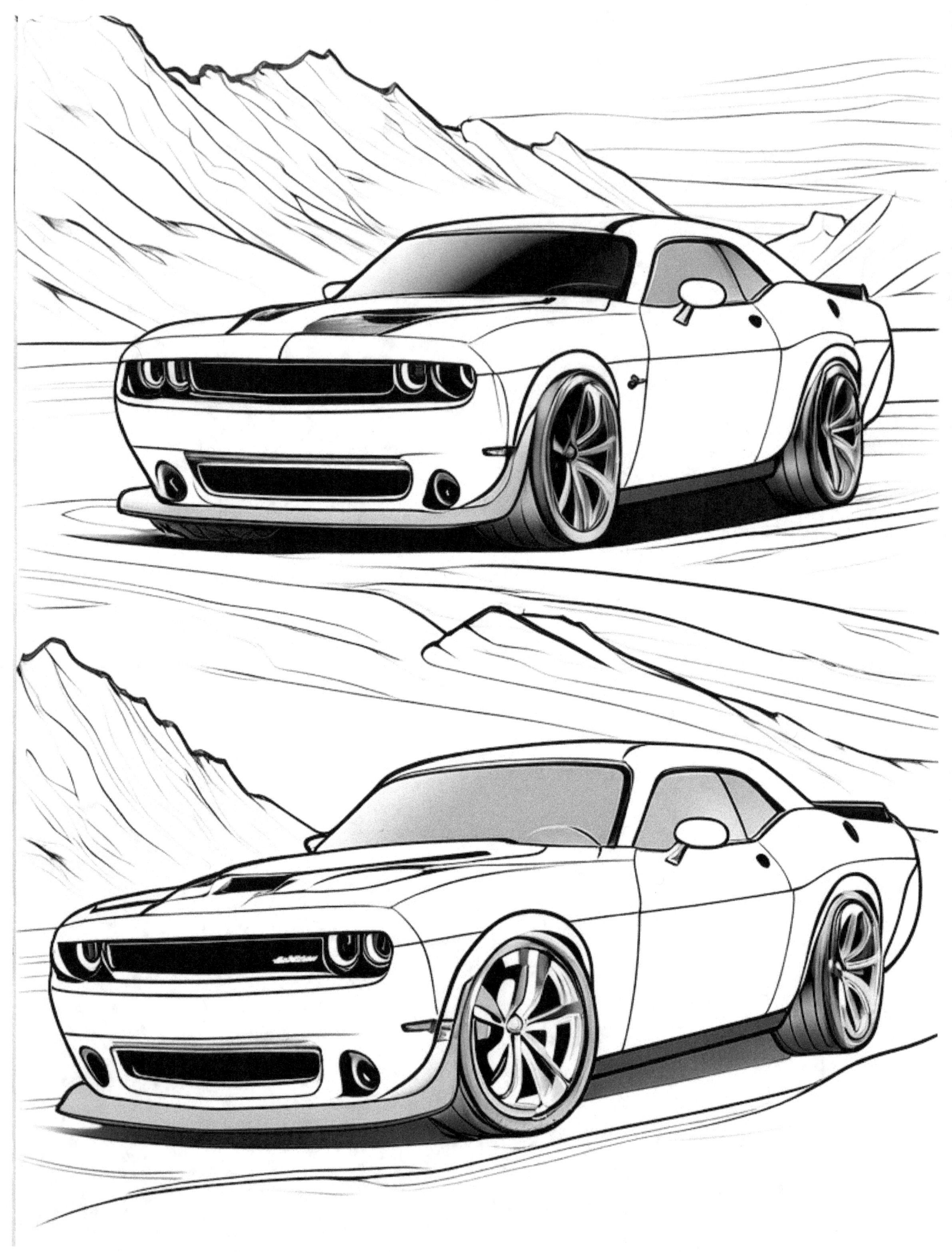

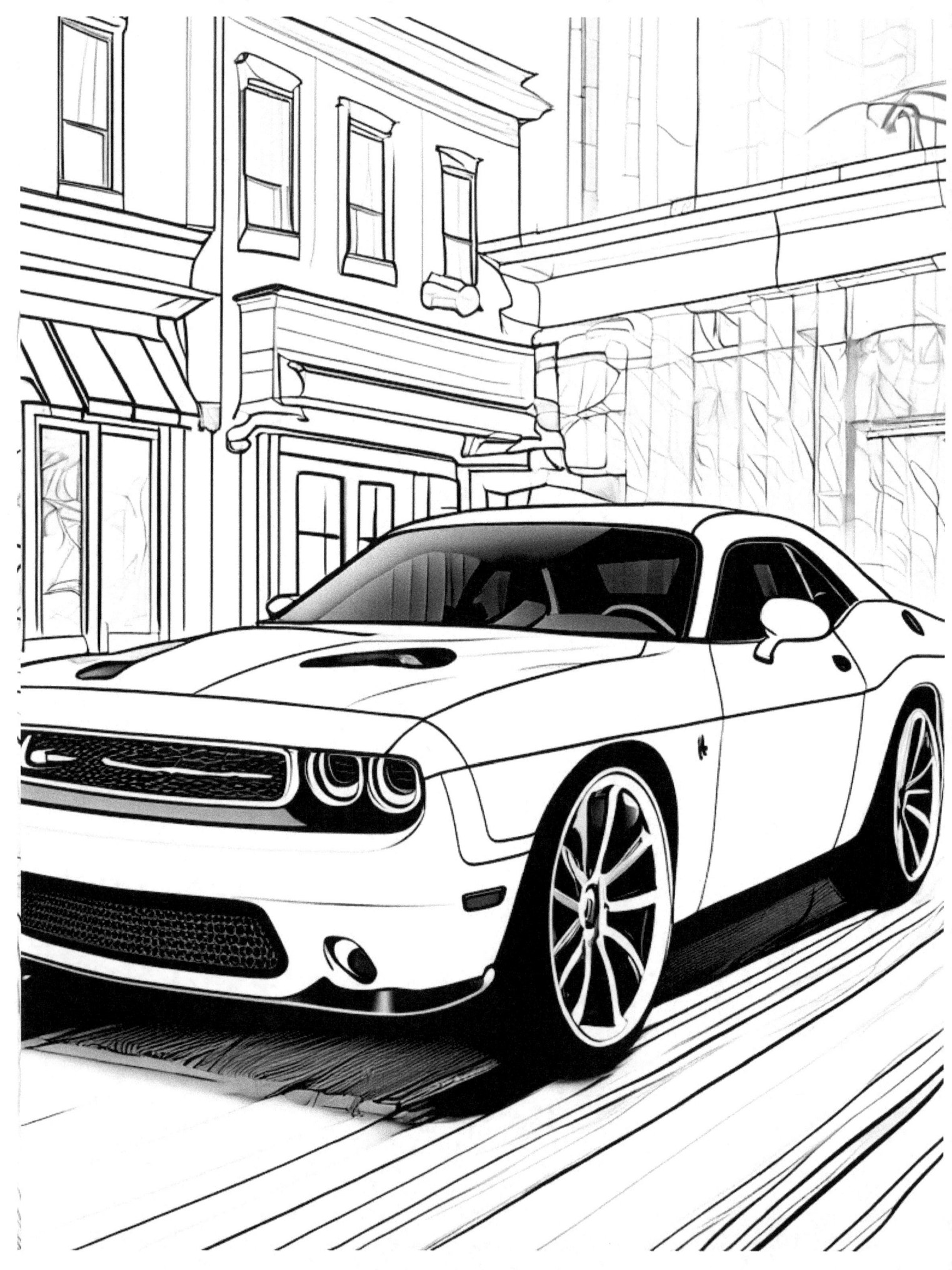

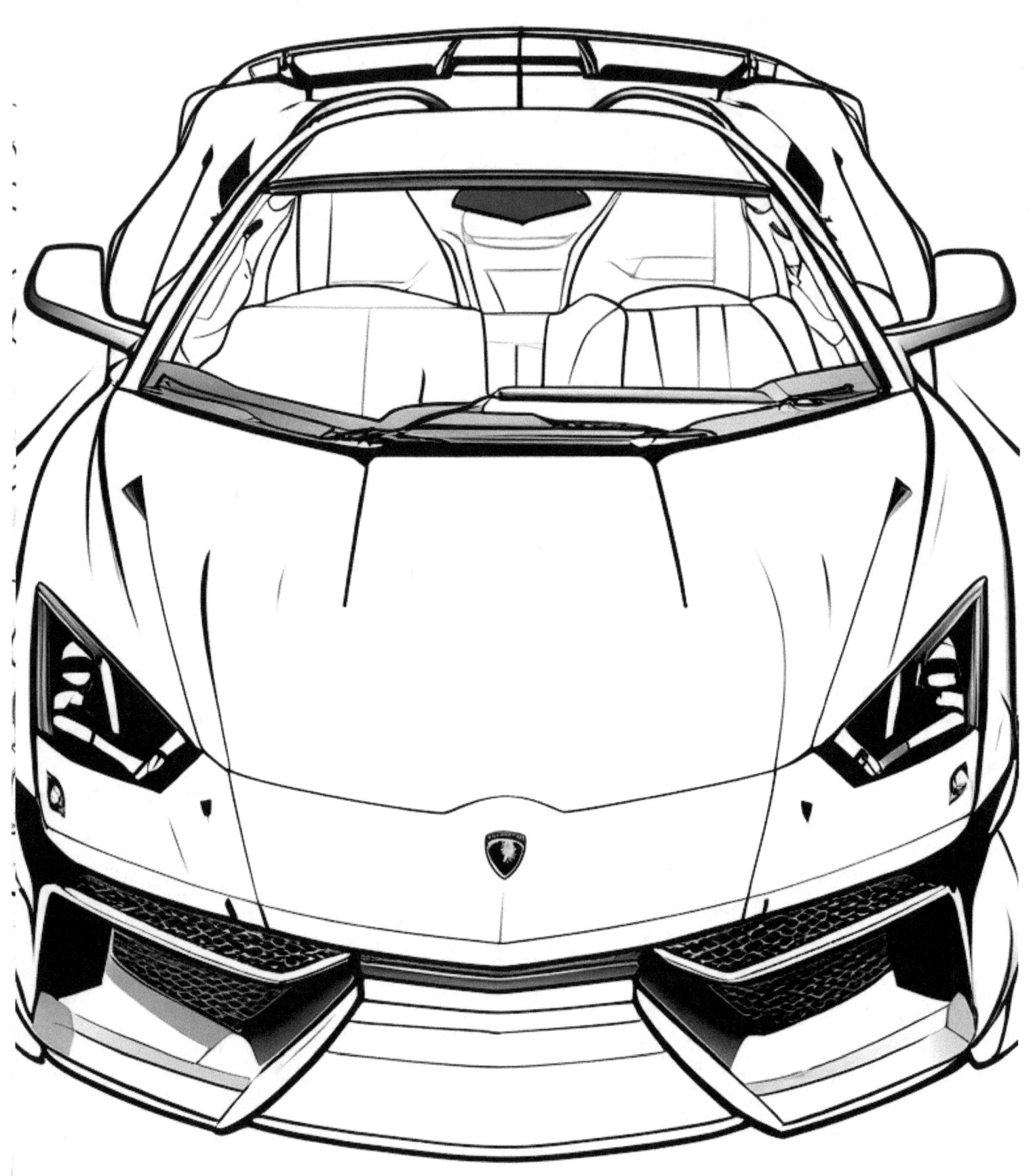

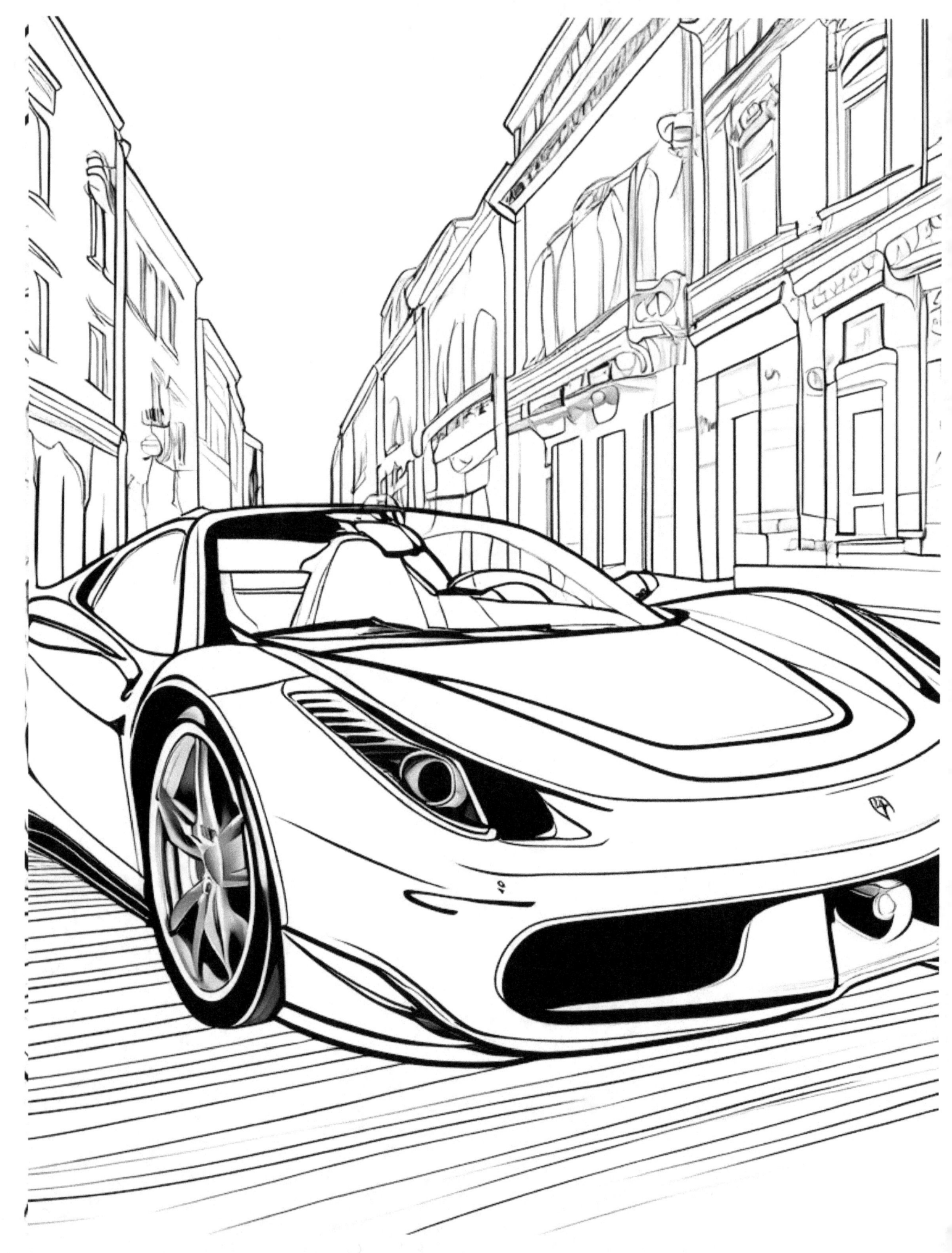

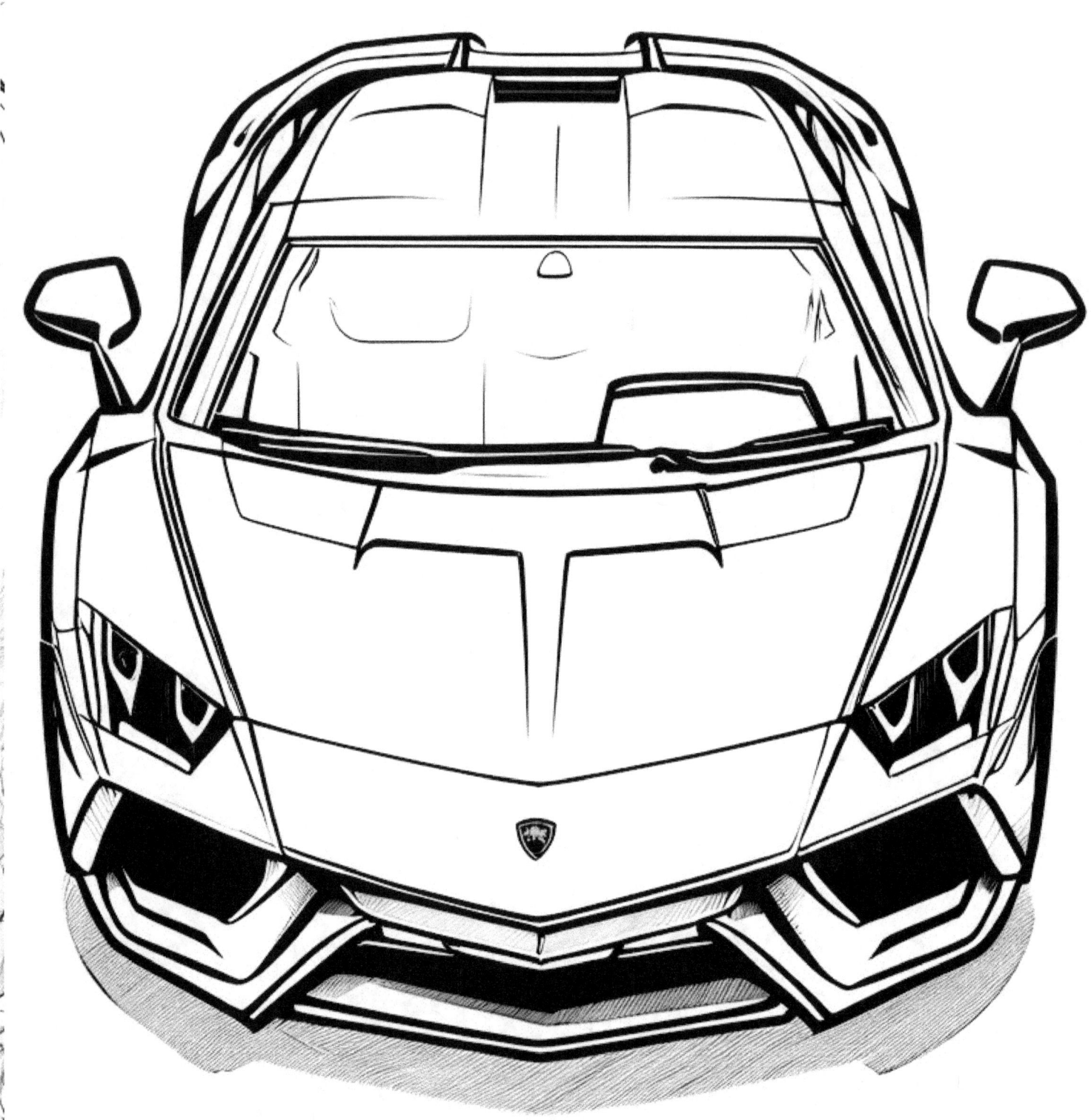

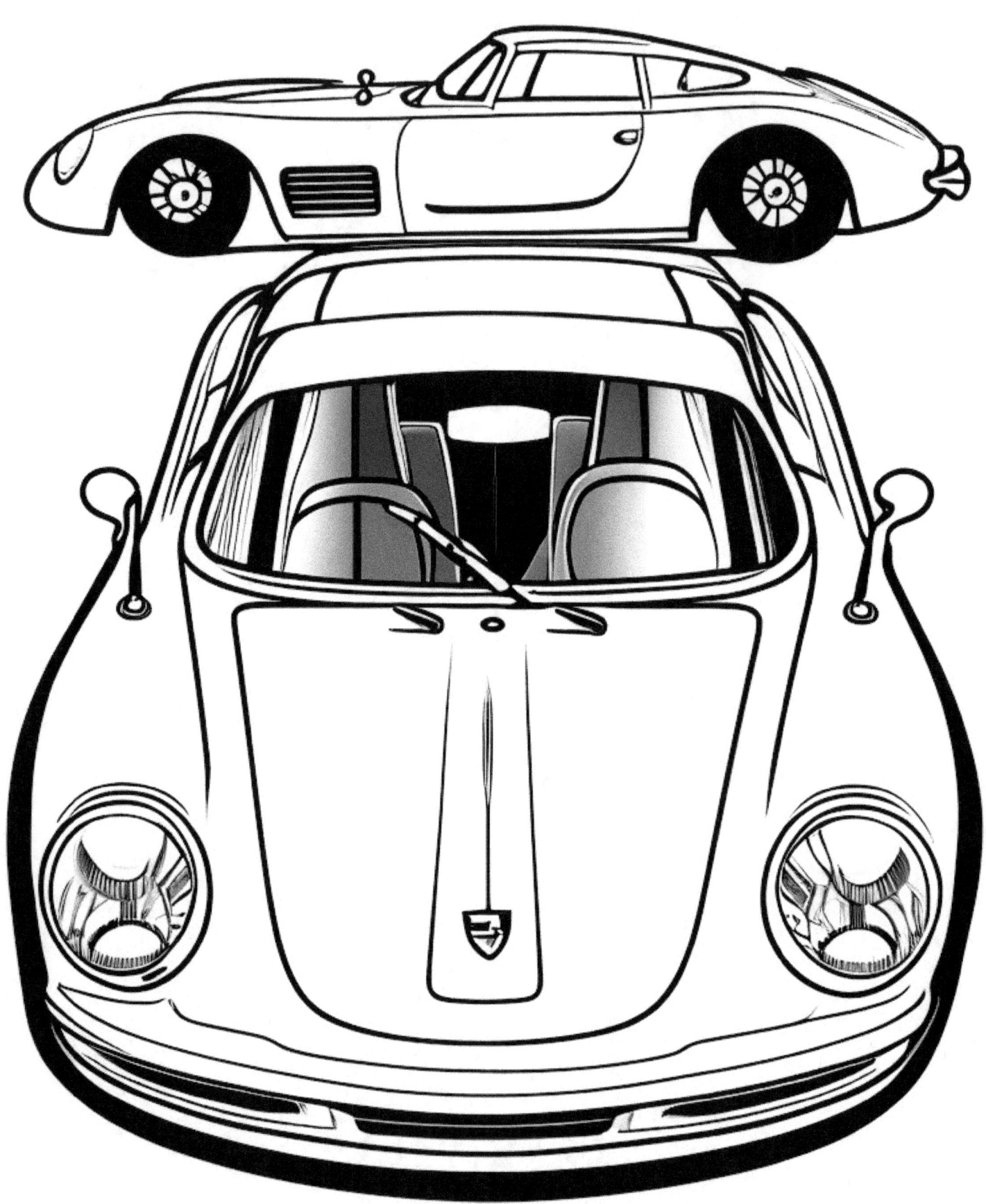

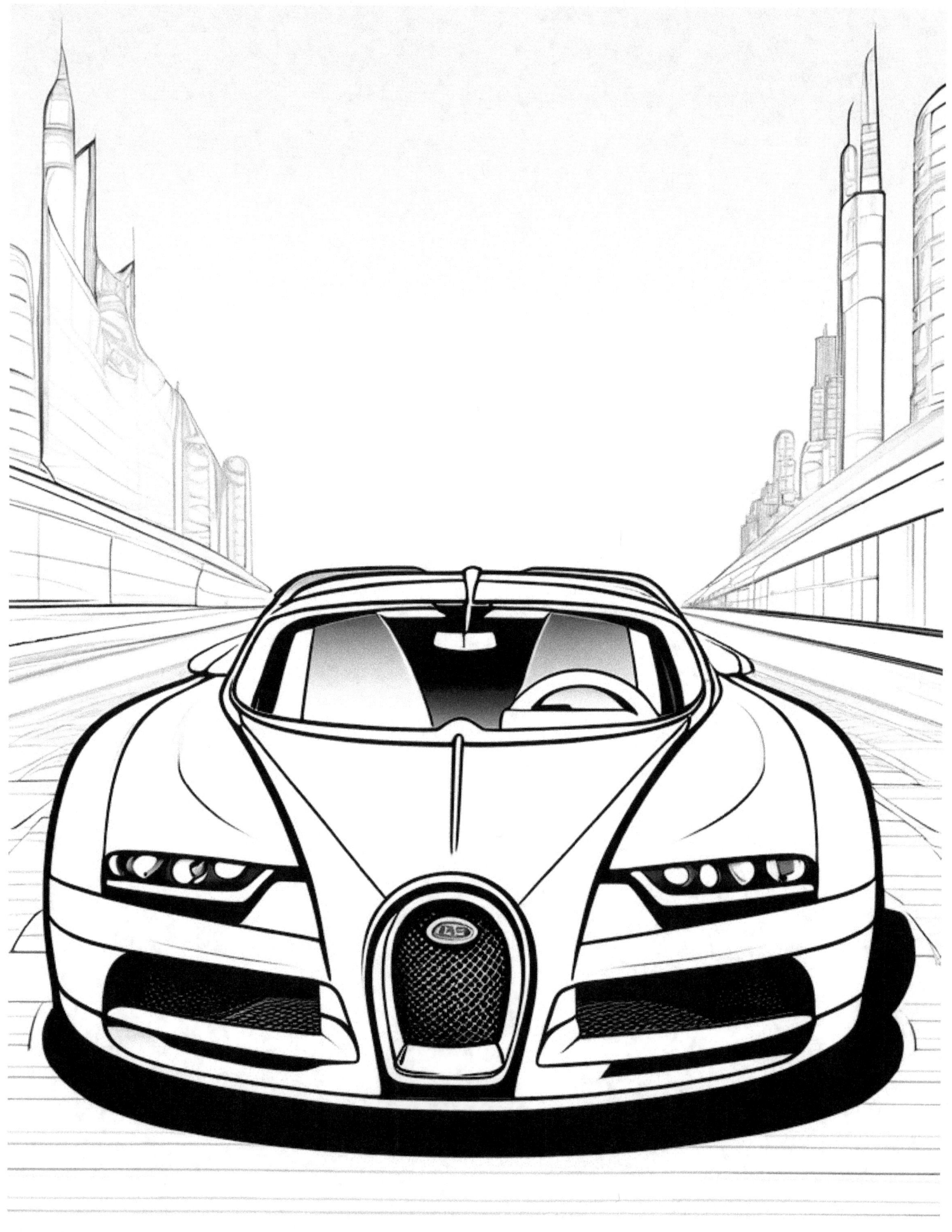

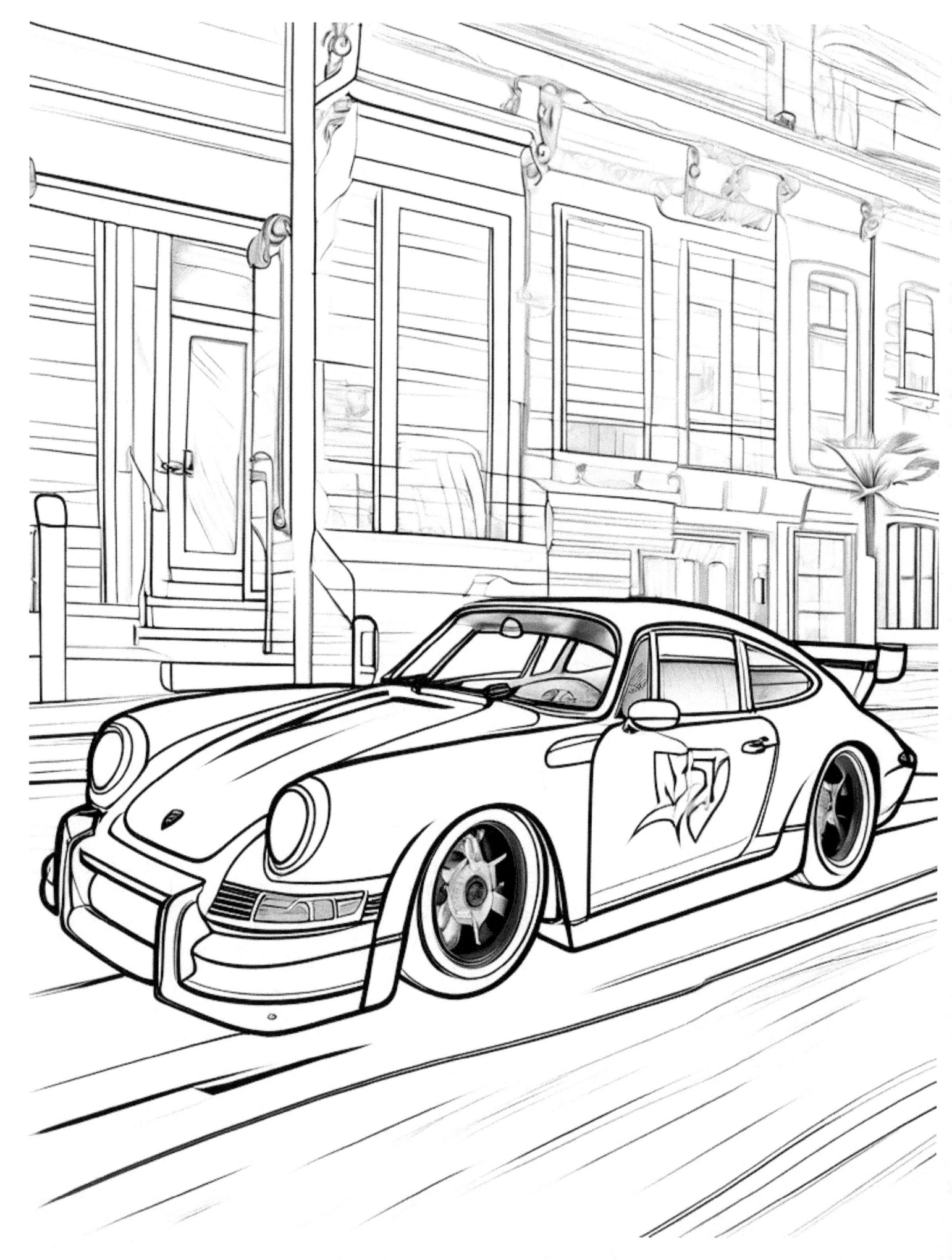

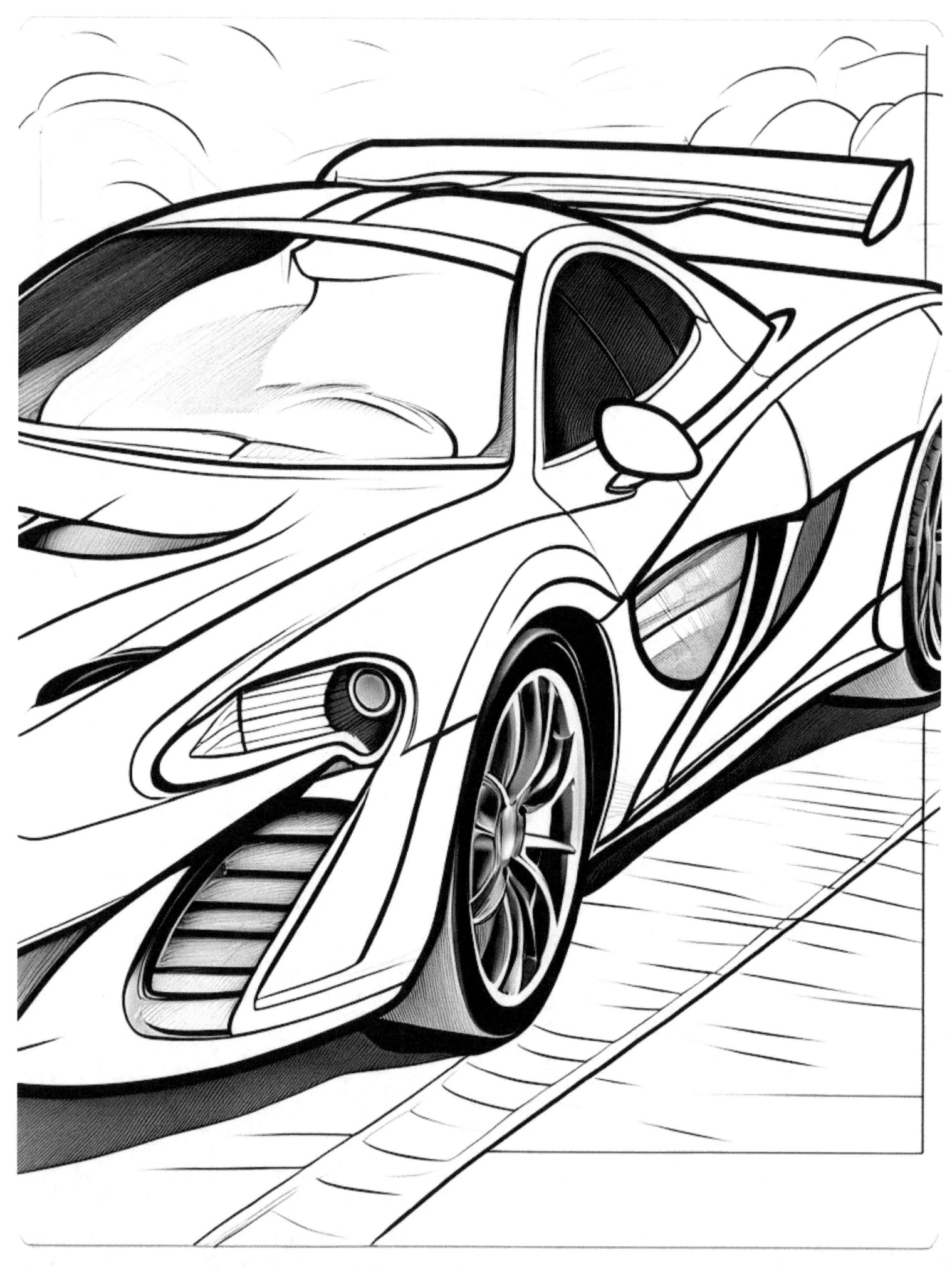

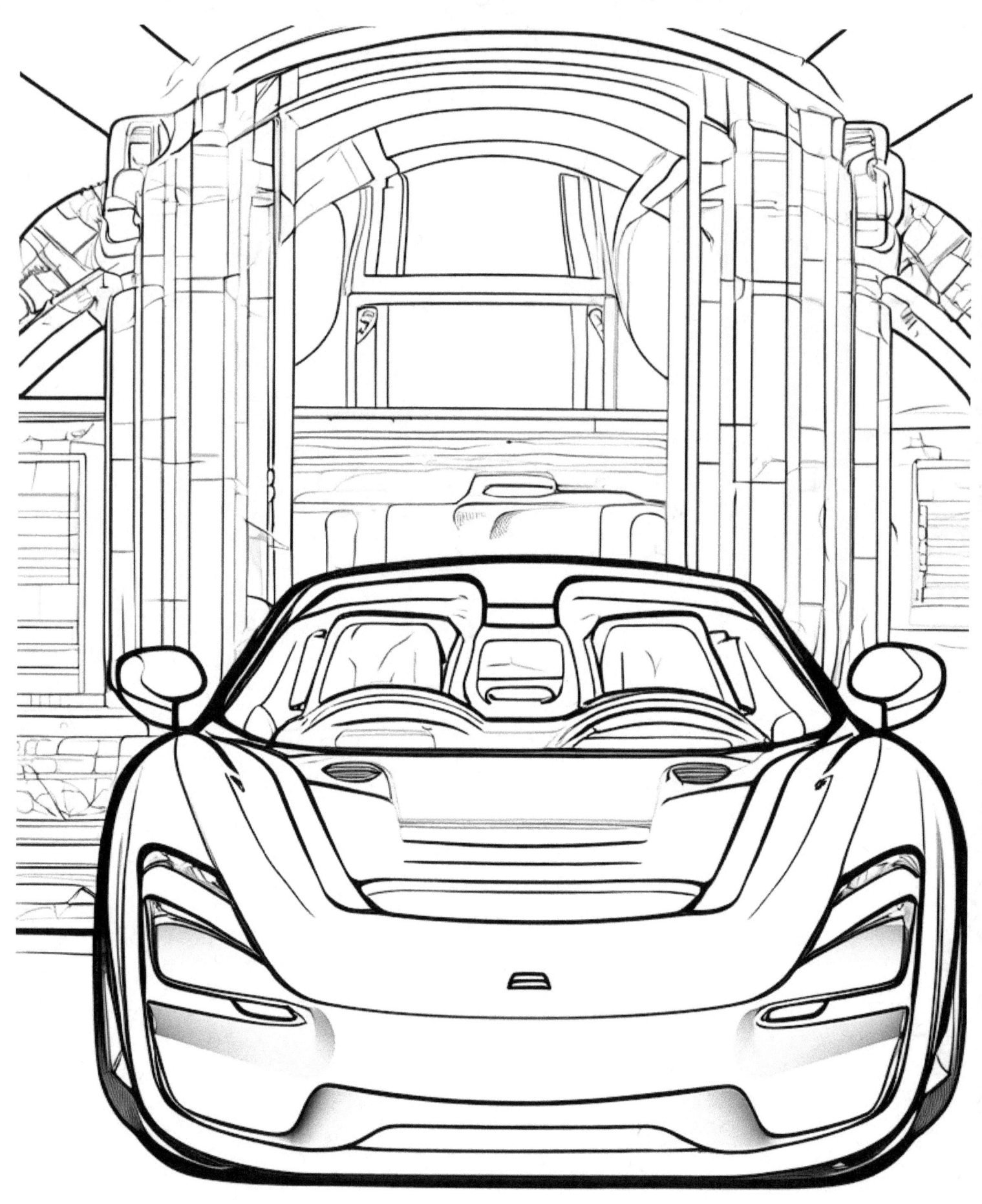

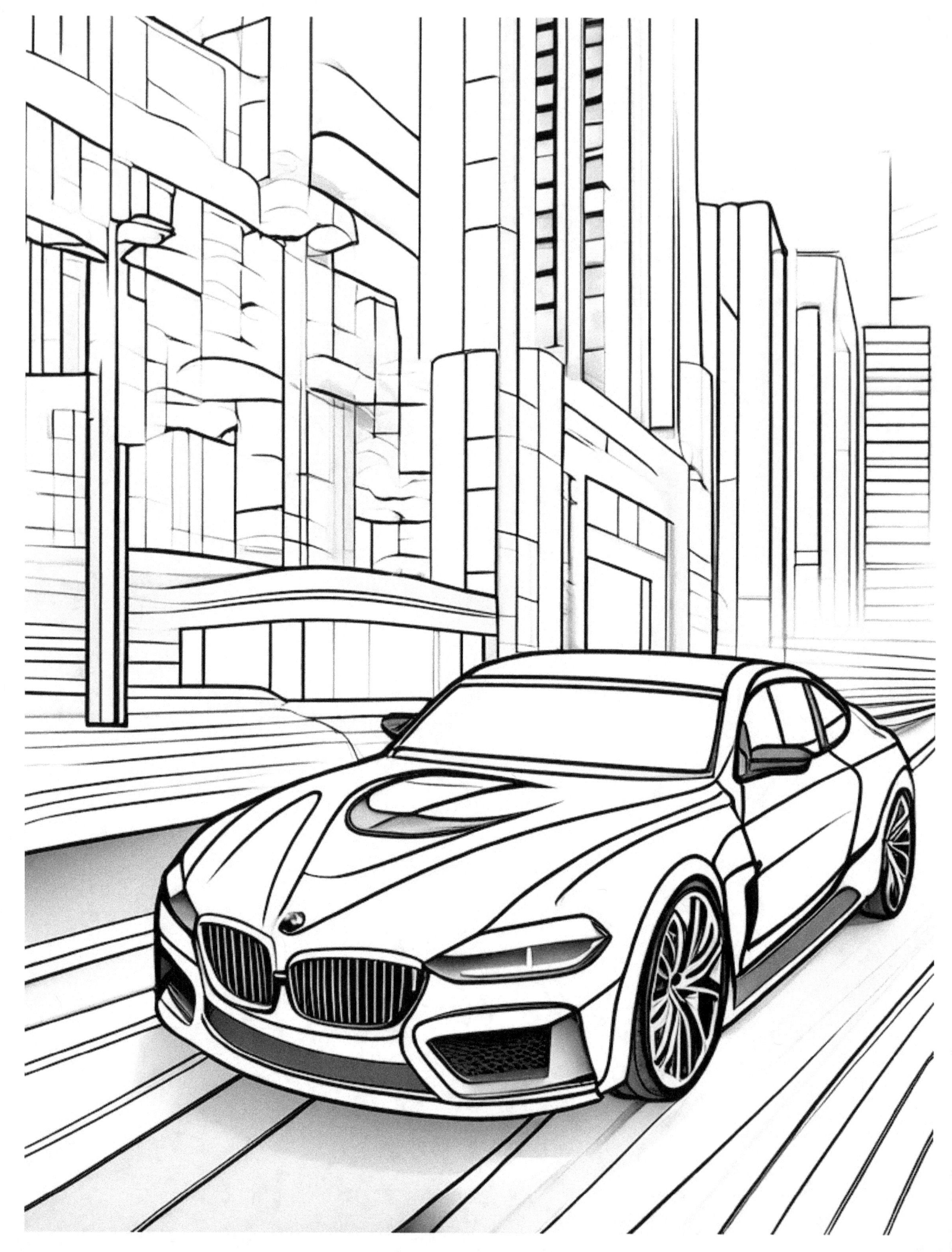

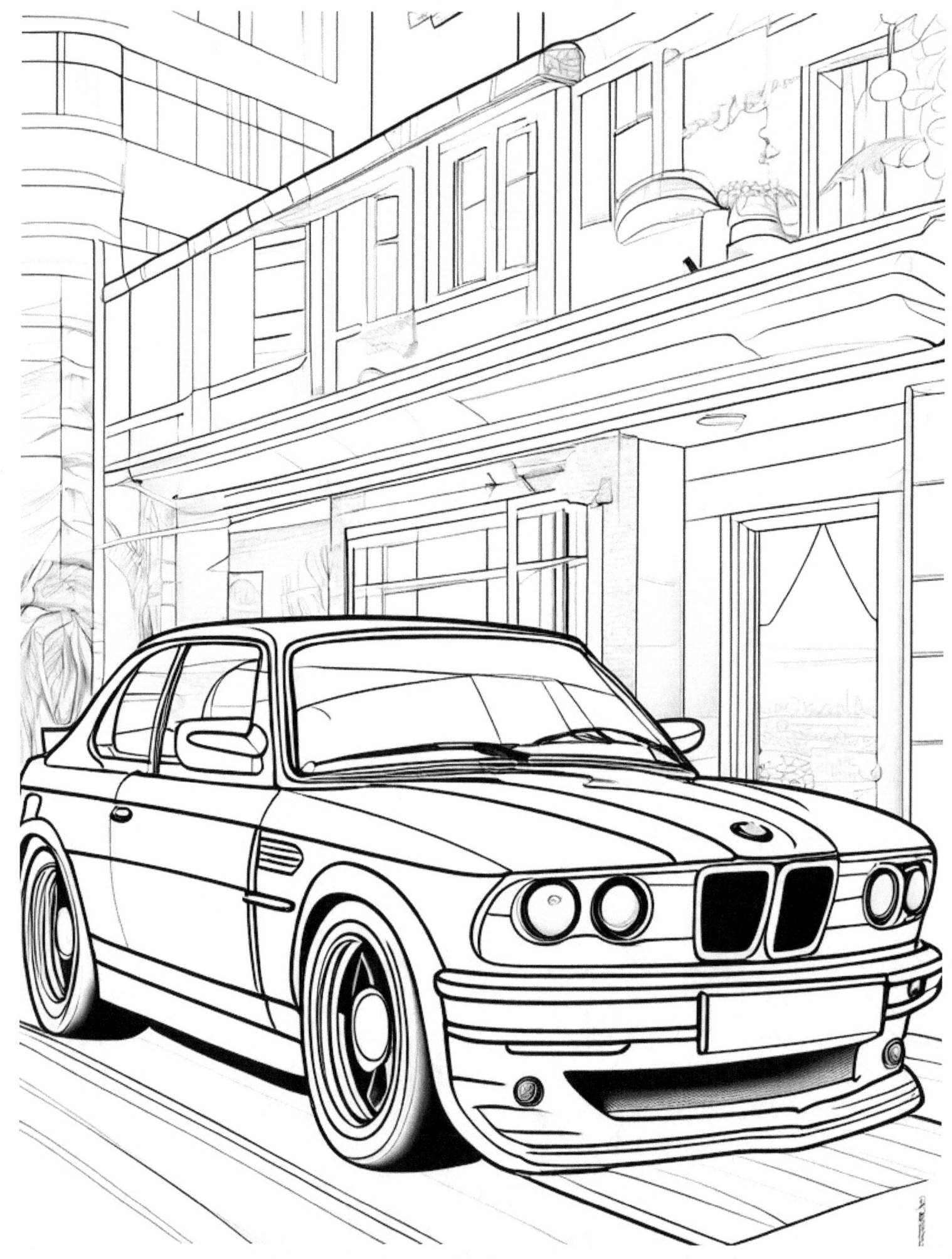

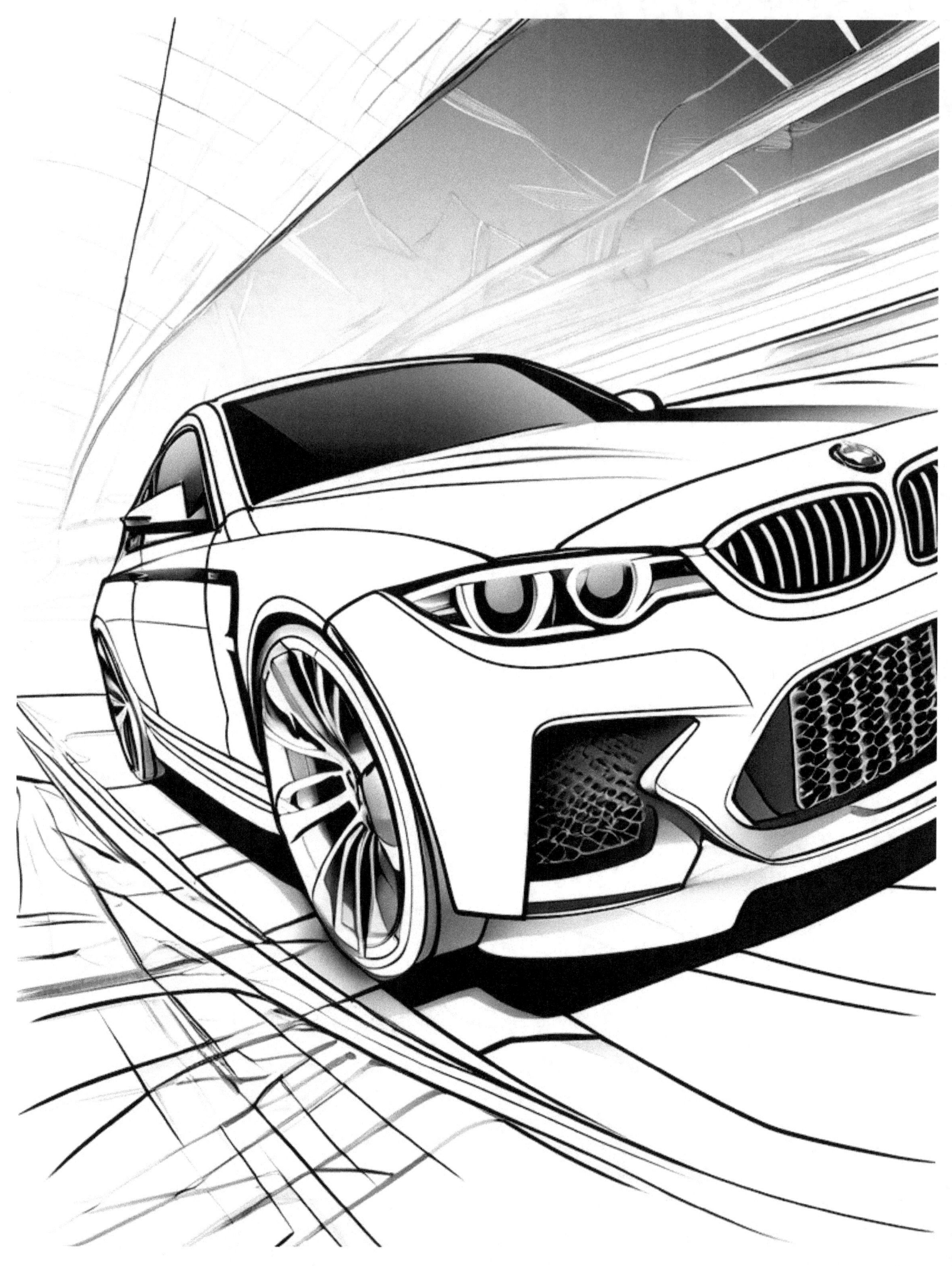

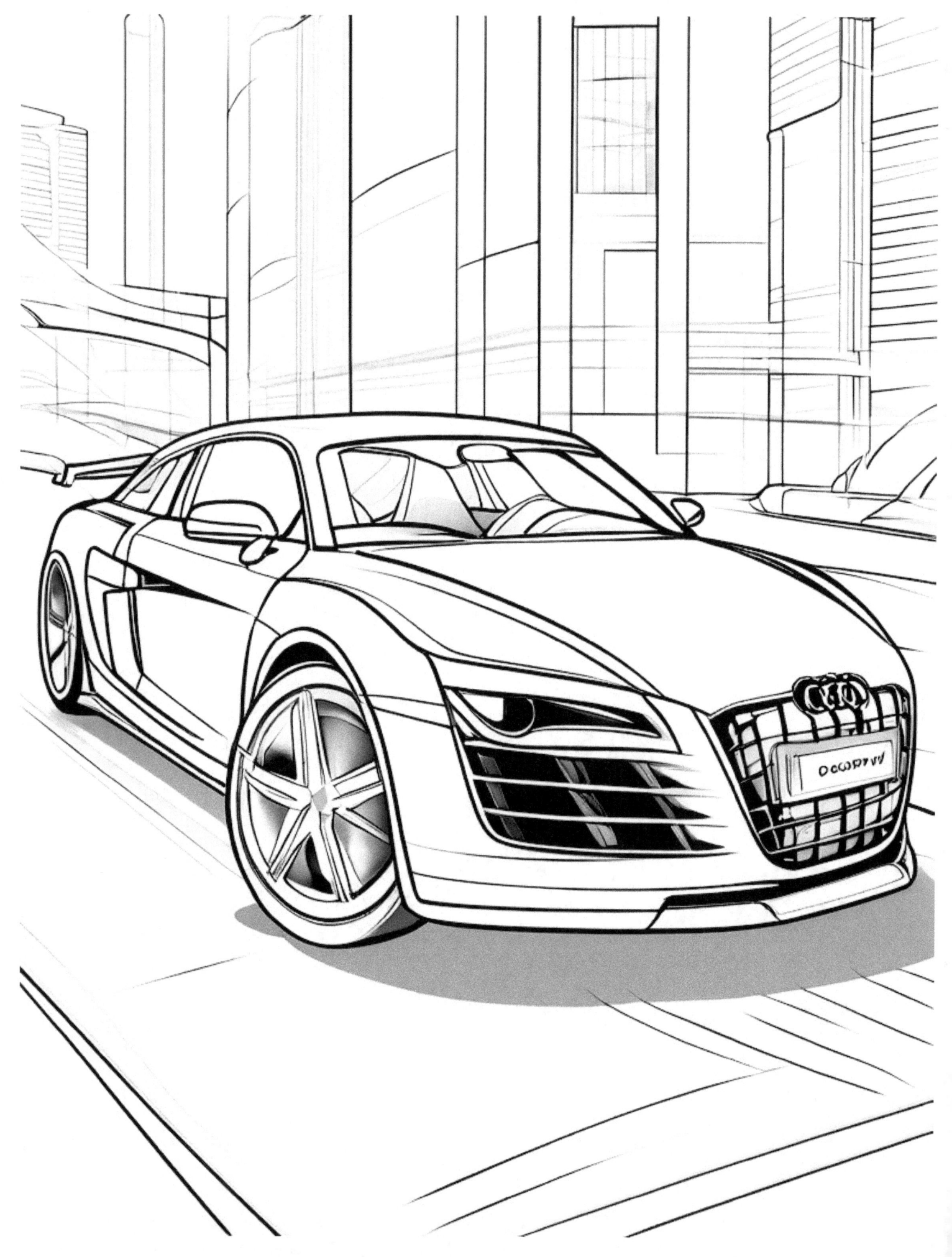

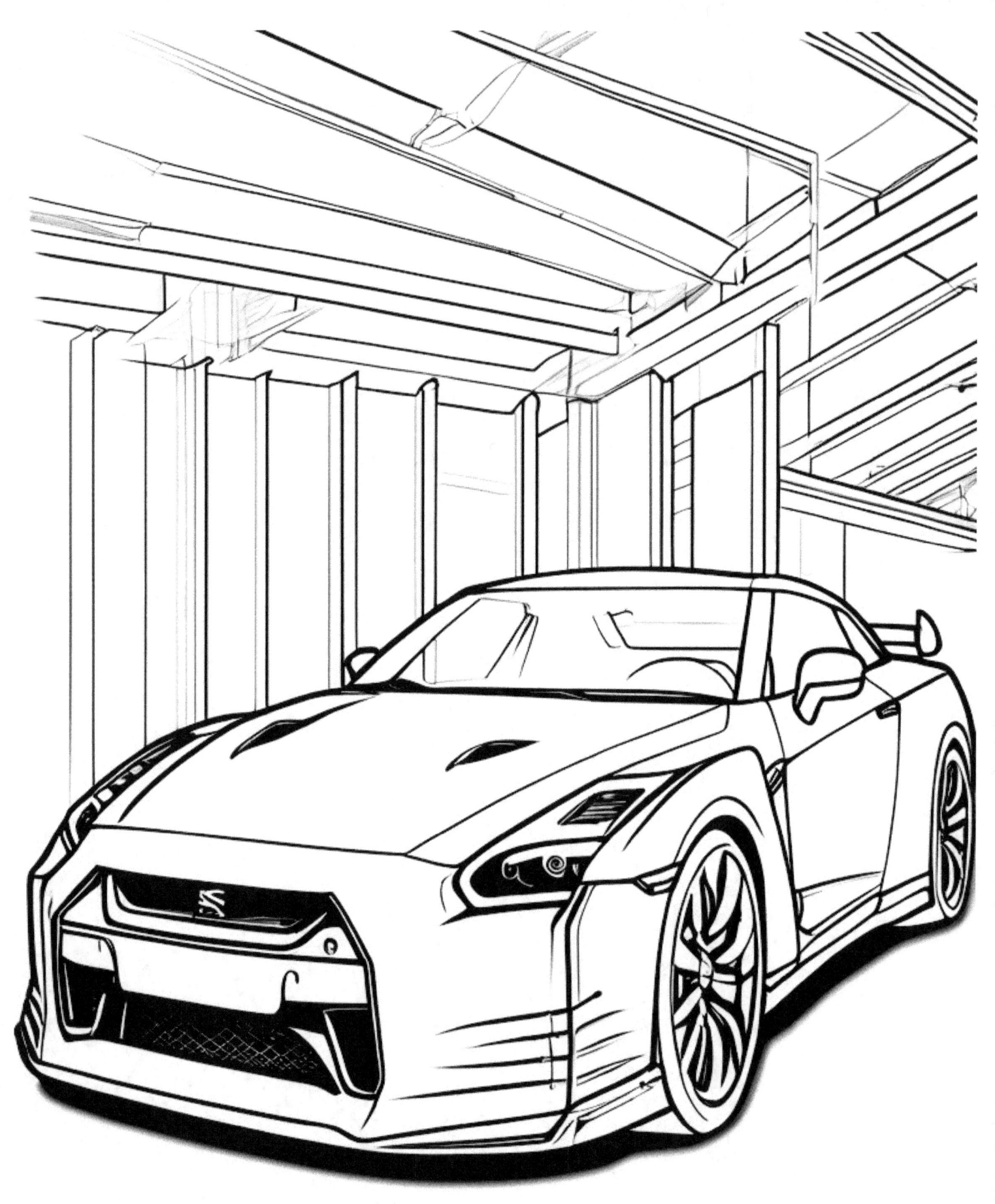

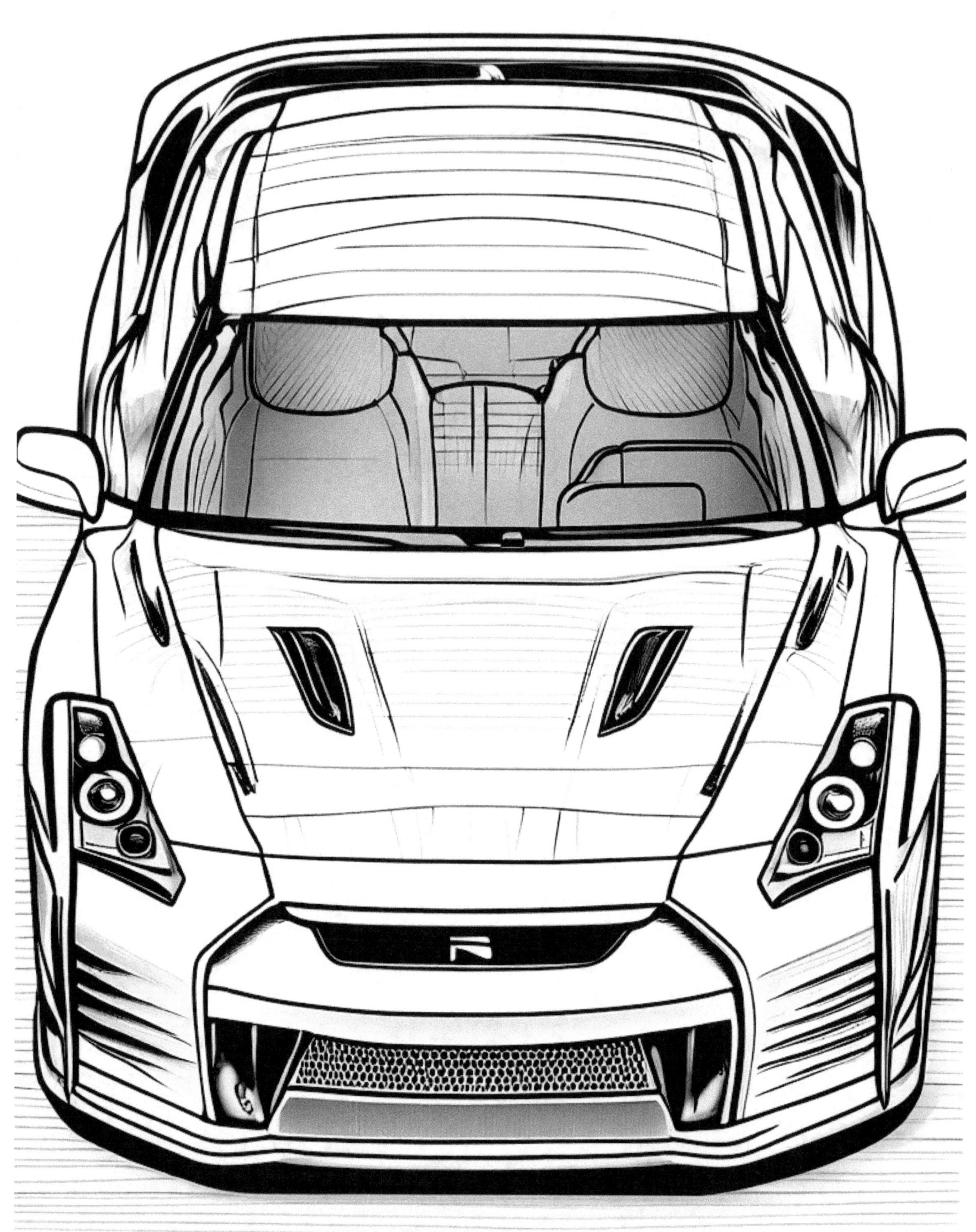

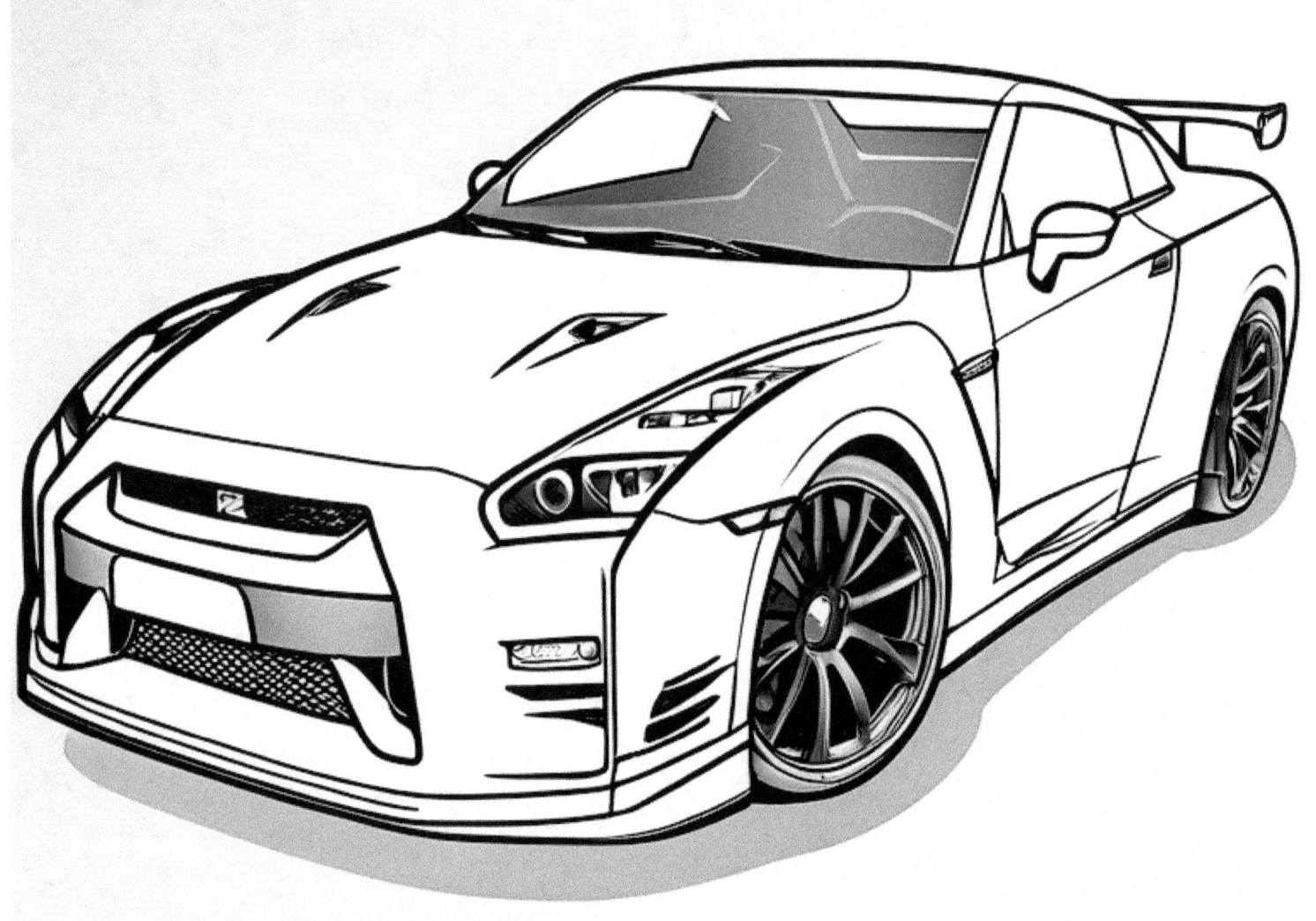

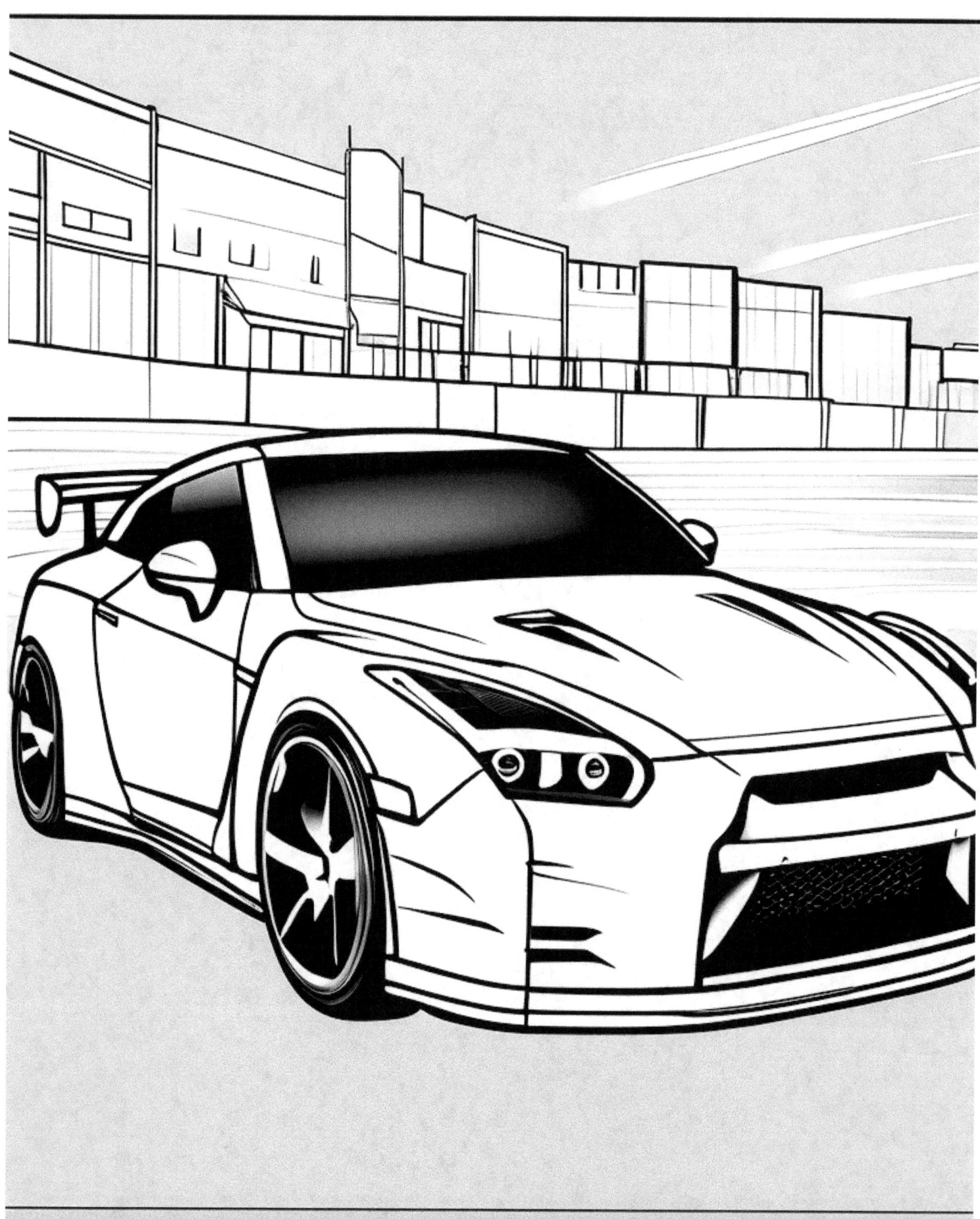

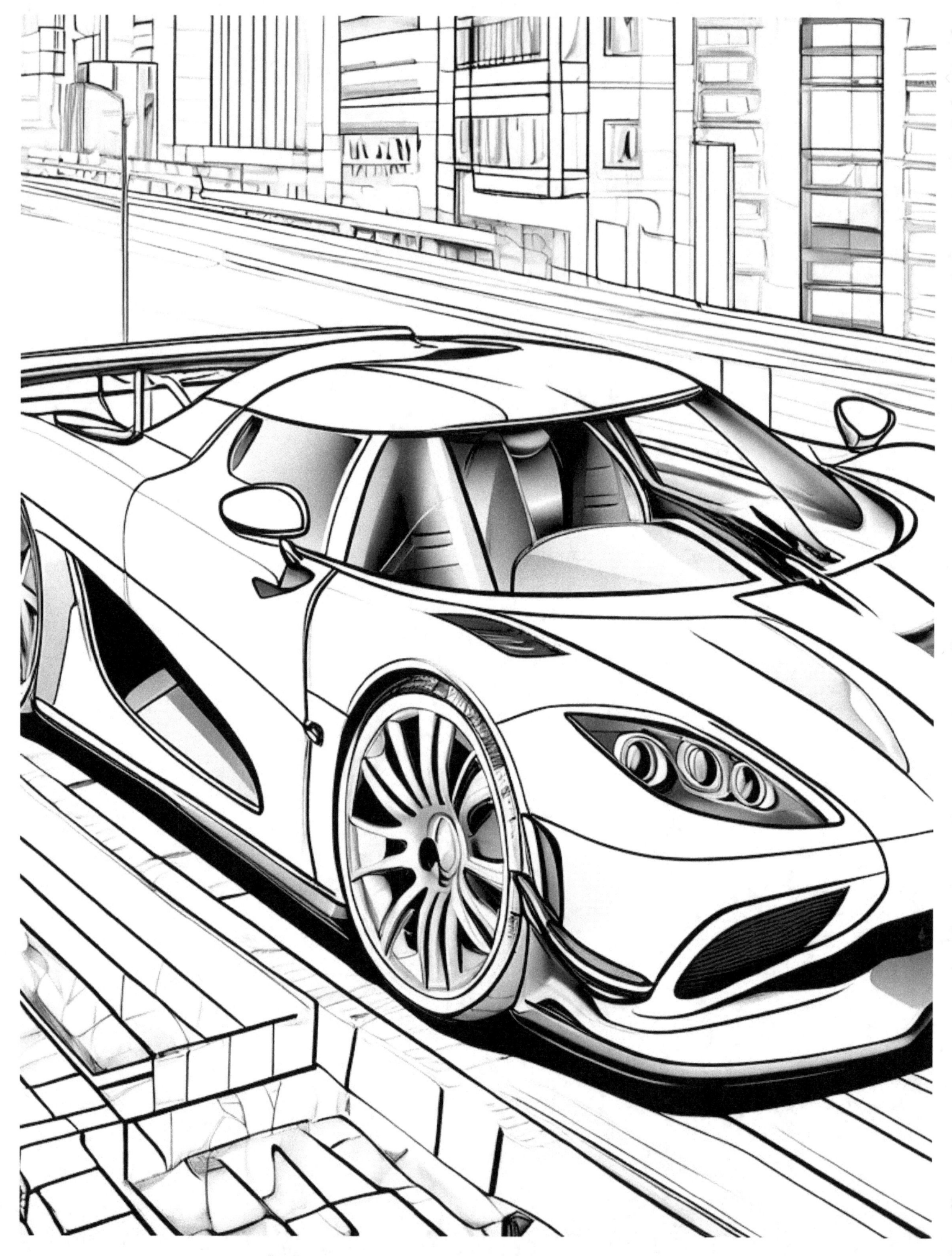

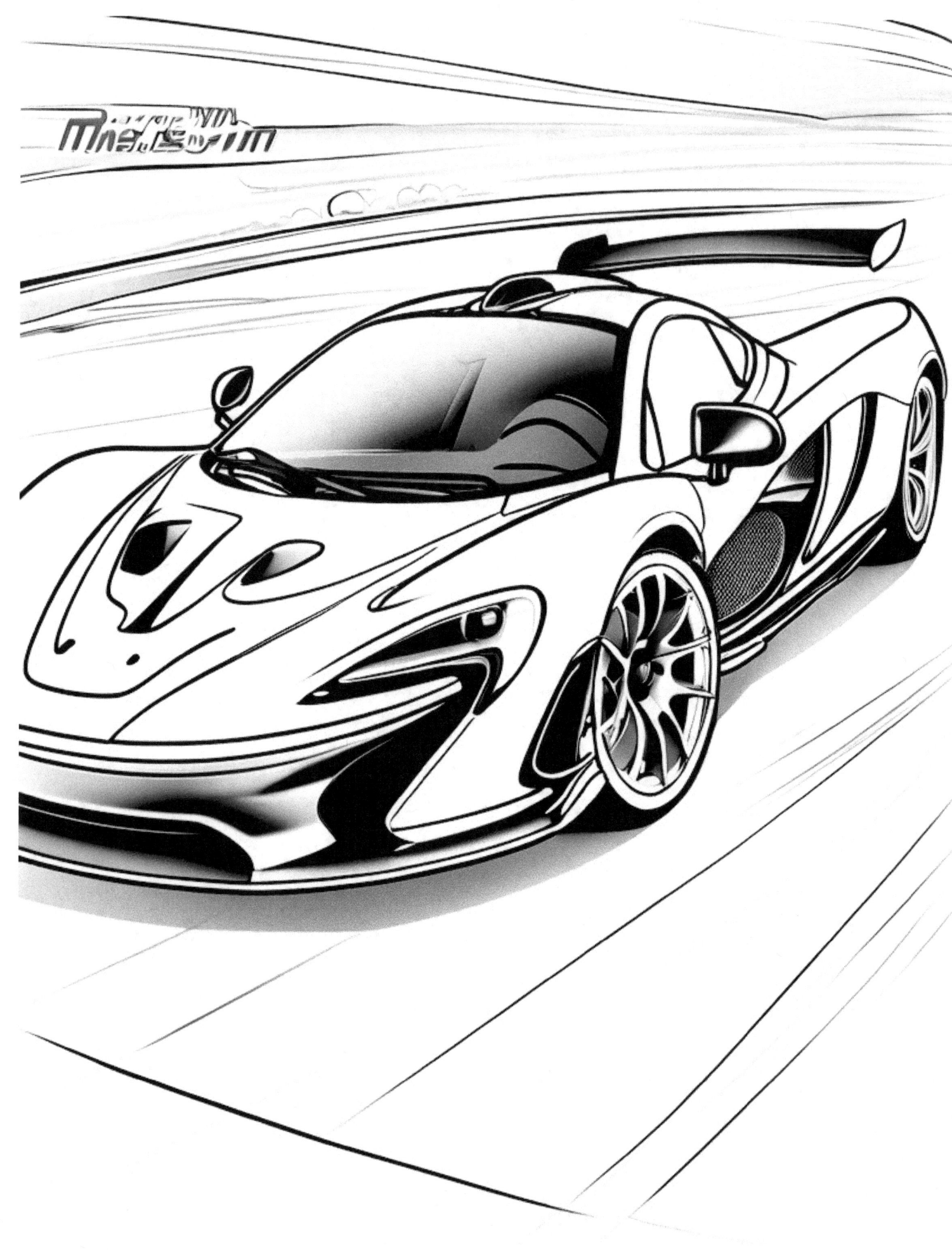

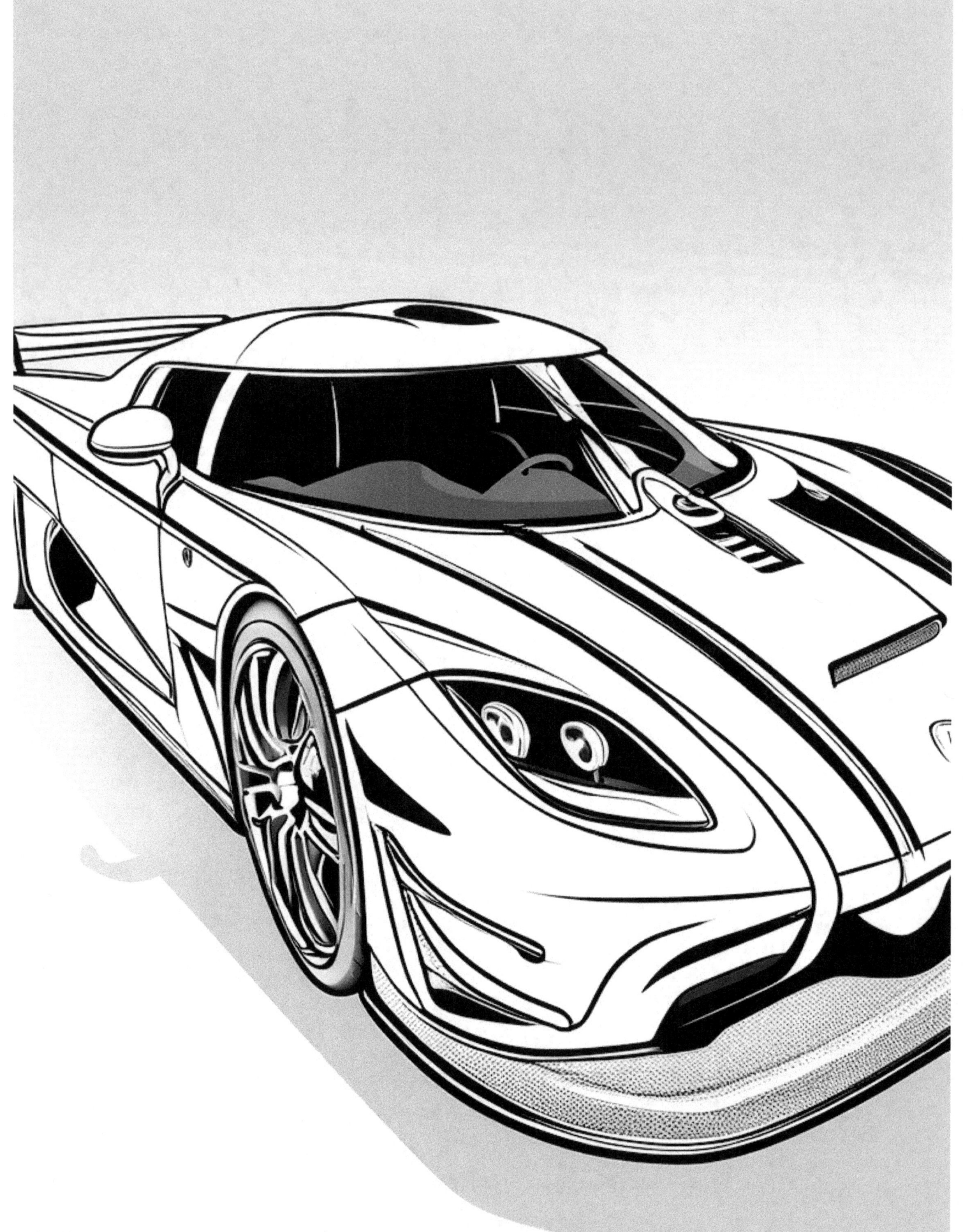

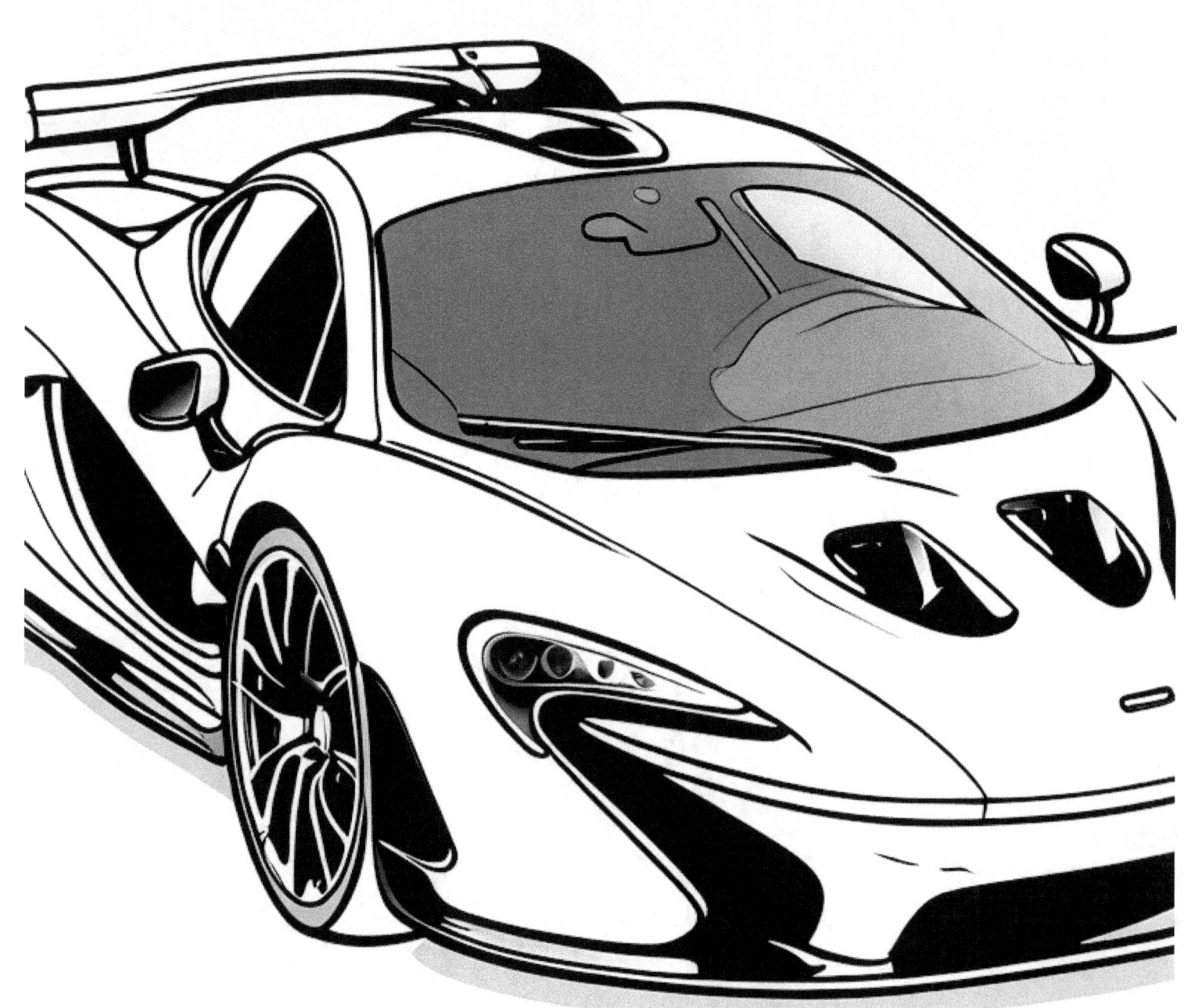

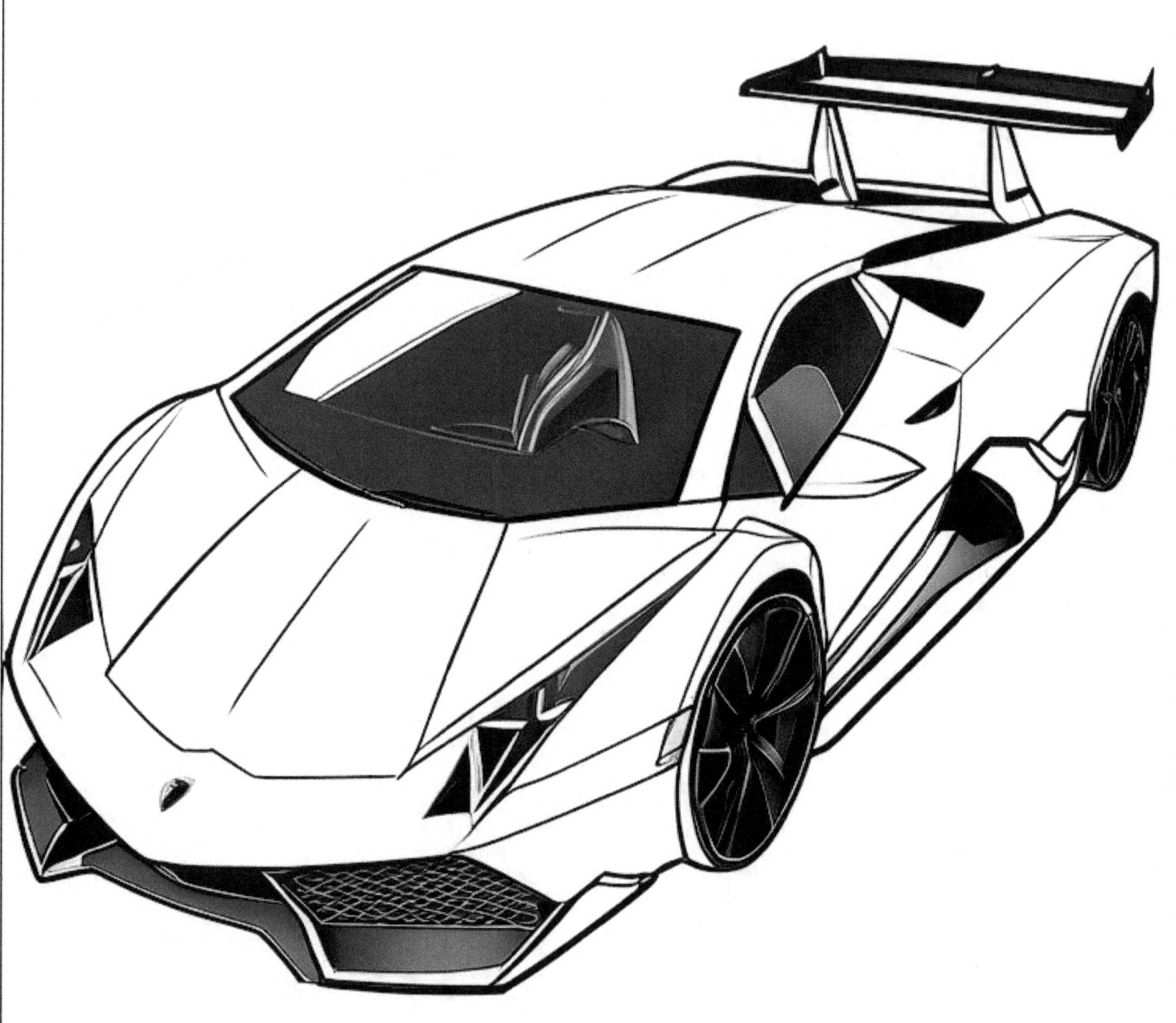

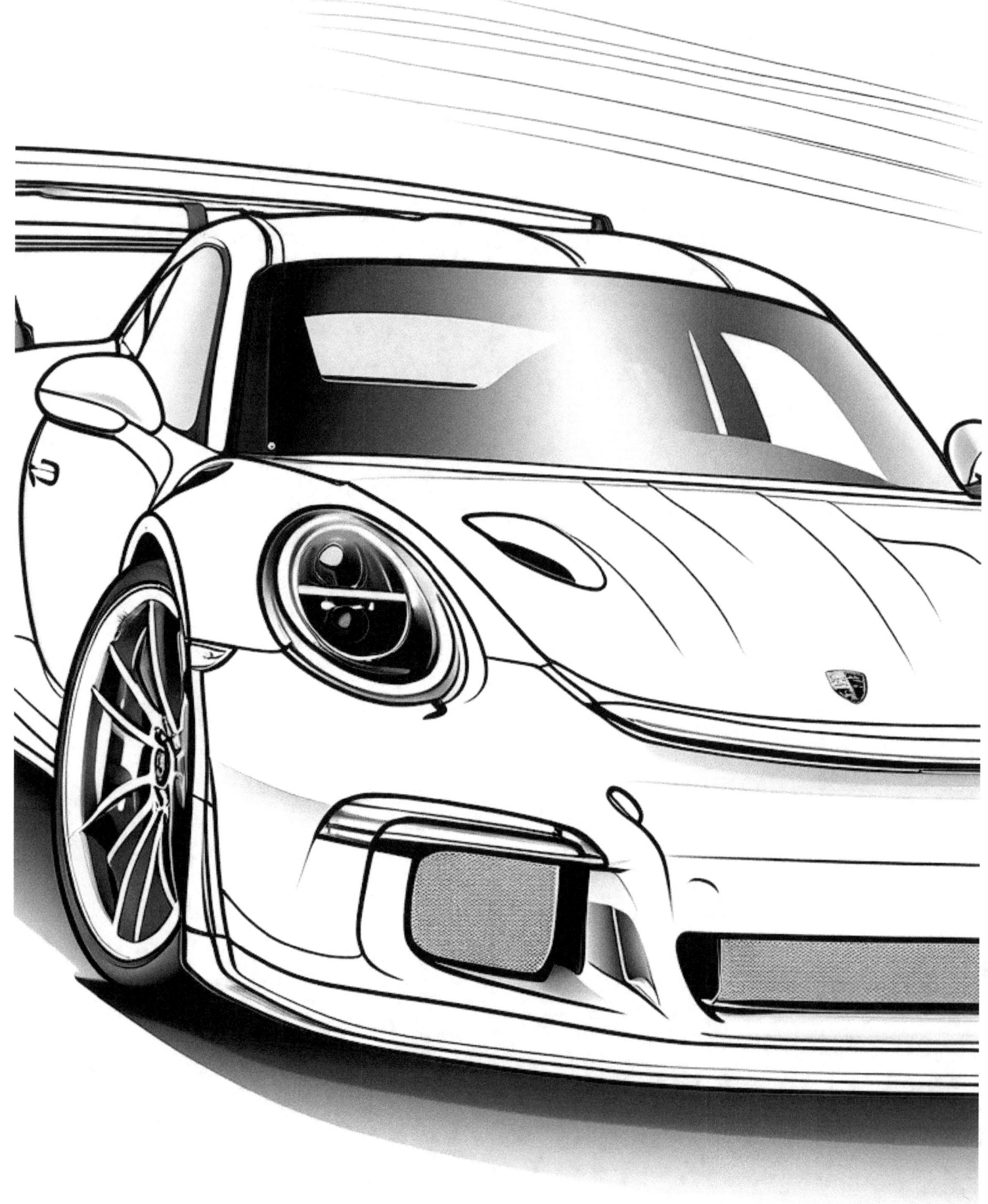

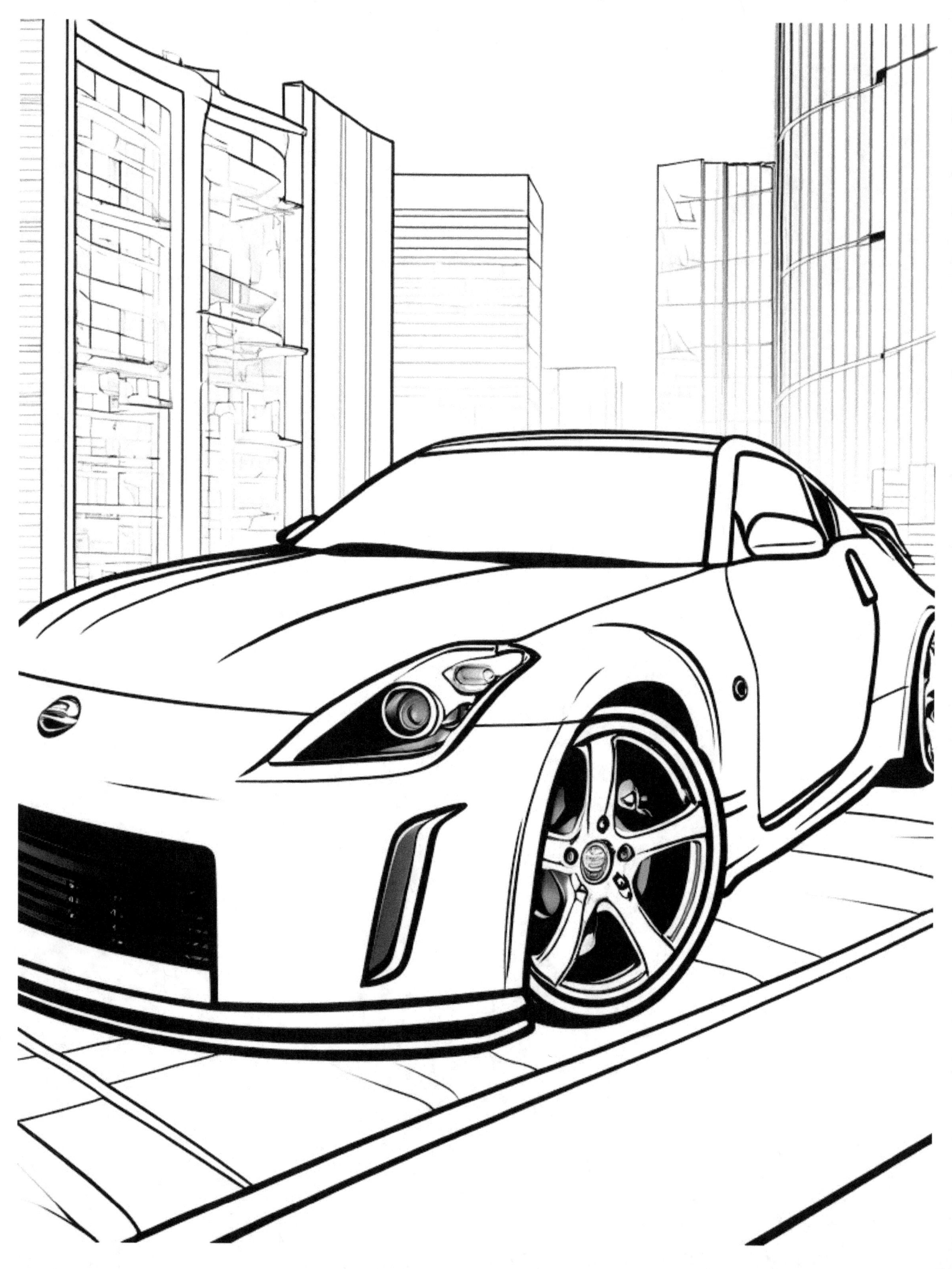

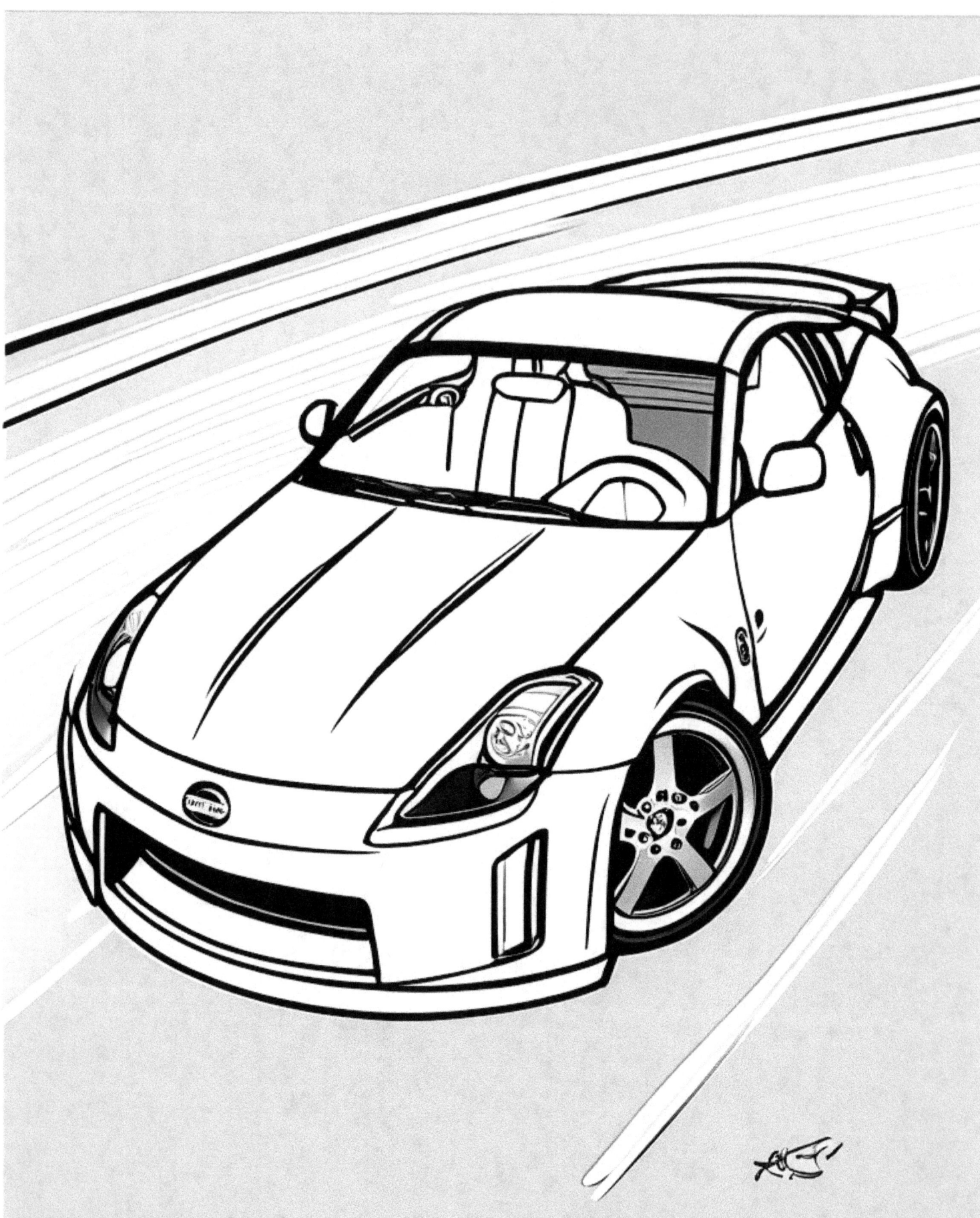

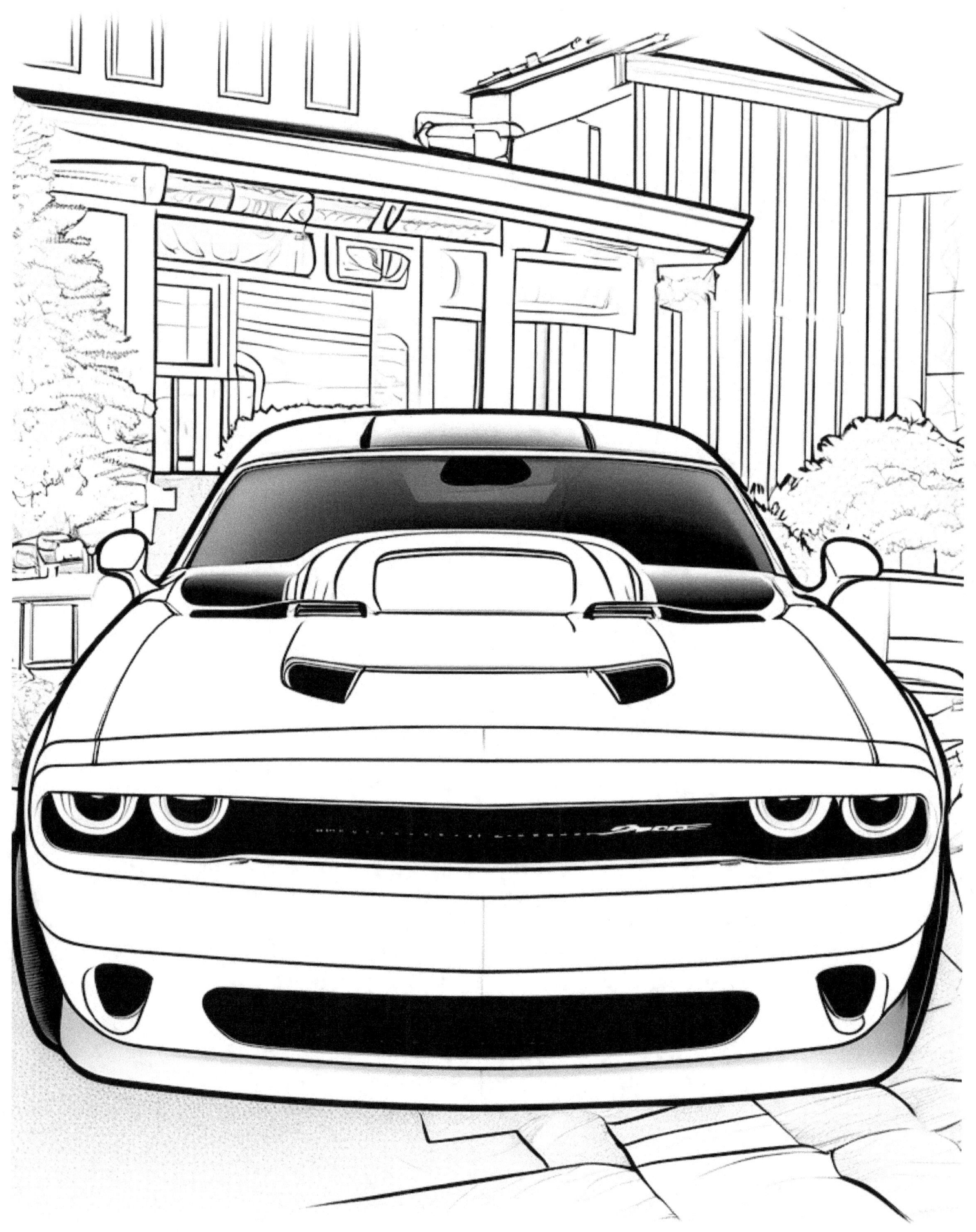

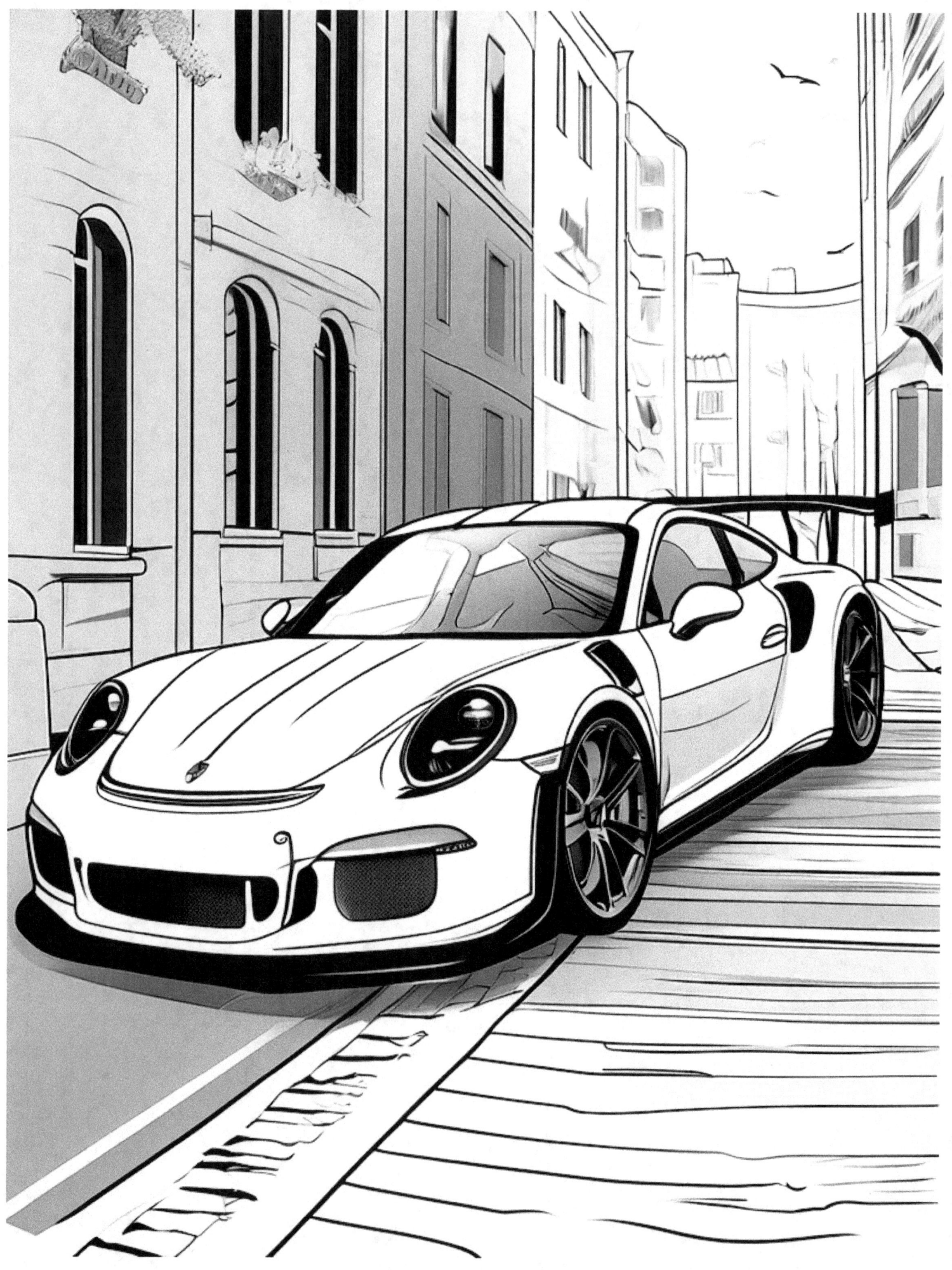

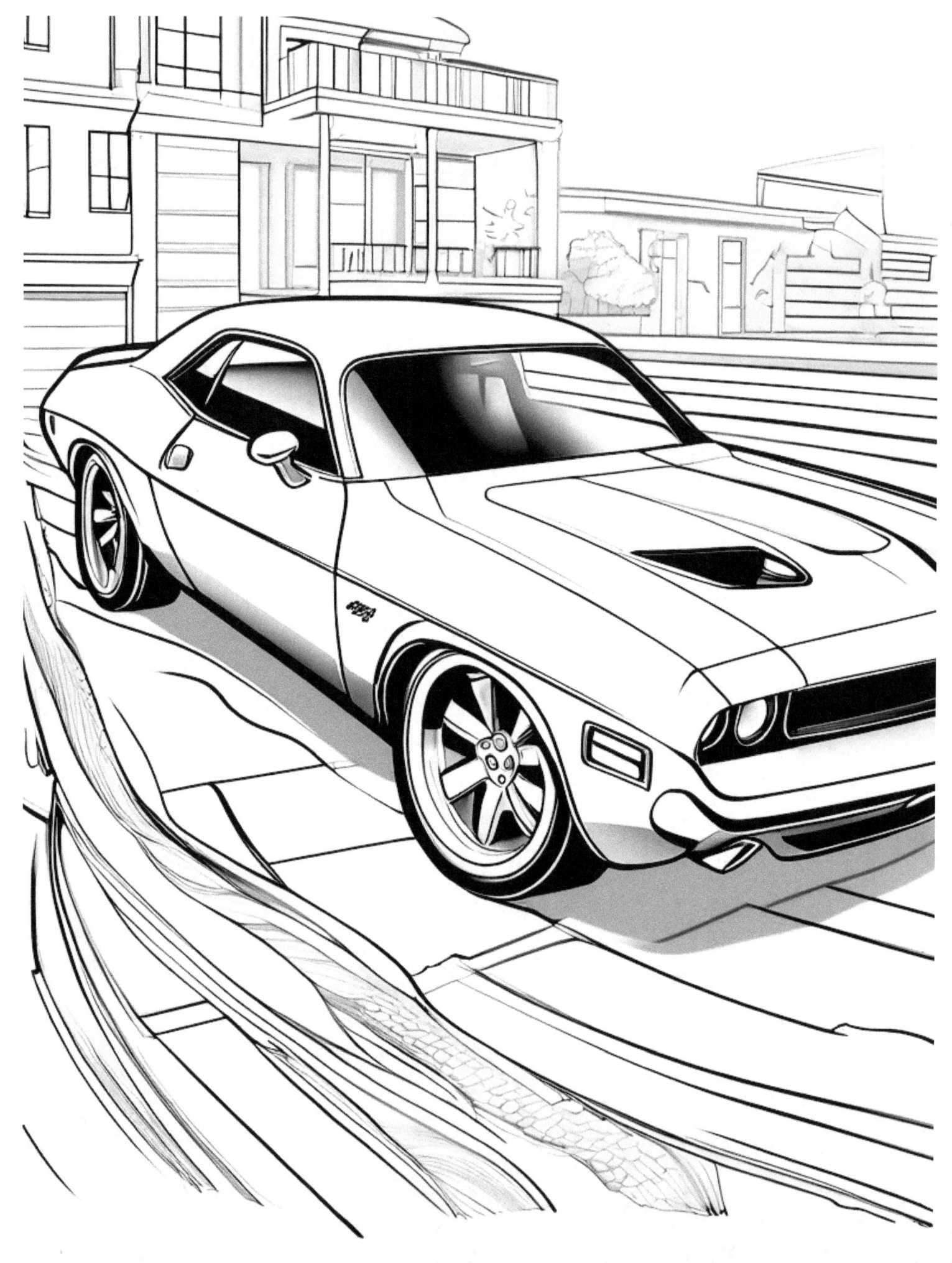